Thrifty Sister

Thrifty Sister

Saving Ways for Black Folks

Pat Worthy Benson

Writers Club Press

San Jose New York Lincoln Shanghai

Thrifty Sister
Saving Ways for Black Folks

Writers Club Press
an imprint of iUniverse, Inc.

For information address:
iUniverse, Inc.
5220 S. 16th St., Suite 200
Lincoln, NE 68512
www.iuniverse.com

ISBN: 0-595-20325-6

Printed in the United States of America

Acknowledgements

I thank God for the talents and blessings bestowed upon me
and His strength that keeps me

I also thank my sister, Lori
for her consistent support, encouragement and belief in me
and the thrifty lifestyle

Contents

Foreword

Some Words of Wisdom

Readers are advised to exercise caution and use reasonable, personal judgment when using any tips or remedies in this book. I have personally used, tried and tested these thrifty methods without any adverse effects, however, if there is any doubt or reservations about any advice stated, please consult a licensed professional on the matter before proceeding. It is up to each reader to determine their personal level of safety, and any advice should be weighed against the reader's own abilities and circumstances and applied accordingly. Thank you.

Chapter 1: The Thrifty Sister

Please don't call me cheap, call me thrifty. Thrifty Sister, that is. Thrifty living is an attitude, a state of mind. Wouldn't you like to learn how to improve the quality of life for you and your family—on the same amount of money your currently earn? It is possible. Learning this frugal art will get you out of debt and out of the dumps. Once you begin to experience the joys of thrifty living, you'll never want to return to your old ways again.

Making provisions for the future while managing your immediate needs can be a difficult juggling act if you don't have the proper tools. Thankfully, the tools you need don't have to be bought; you already have them! Discover how to tap into your own creativity and sharpen your instincts. Find a comfortable balance that's easy to maintain. You can start with baby steps or take big giant steps, depending on your personal preference or need. I'll show you how to begin your own personal journey to prosperity through frugality.

I am reaching out to my brothers and sisters who are trying to make it day by day, by any means necessary. Often we agonize alone, ashamed to let others know how hard we are struggling. Its time to realize that sharing our struggle strengthens and supports not only the individual, but also the collective whole.

What really needs to be explored is what drives us to spend so much on things that mean so little? If you or a loved one were lying in a hospital bed, how many of your material possessions would give you comfort? It reminds me of a story I once heard about a very rich man that owned the largest estate in town. His home was a storehouse of expensive items he collected over the years. He lived his life in material luxury without much use for friends and family. When he died, all the town folk wanted to know how much money he left behind, (not that any of them were in the will). The clergy who gave his eulogy to an almost empty funeral parlor answered the question quite simply. "He left it ALL!" That's right, you can't take it with you.

It's not surprising many African-Americans still struggle with the same economic issues that have plagued us for decades. Our goals of financial betterment often fall way short of ever reaching fruition. Too many of us are hoping, dreaming, playing lotto and spinning wheels.

Because we live in a capitalistic society, we believe that money will make us happy. With money, we will be able to buy "things". We have been duped into believing the "American Dream" that says owning these "things" will fulfill us. This materialistic attitude sharply differs from our basic African nature. Historically, Blacks relate to one another by family origins and personality, while Whites tend to relate and value their peers according to professional and financial achievements. So much time and energy is spent on making money. It's ironic that once the money is made, many more hours are spent figuring out how to hold on to it.

Listen, I understand we all need a certain amount of cash to afford a decent living. The basics three for the body are food, shelter and clothing. Few Americans are satisfied with this bare minimum, and many would be ashamed to admit that's all they have. But why is it that someone with a meager income can lead a very satisfying, peaceful, fulfilled life, while a rich person can be miserable? It is because the quality of our life is not totally based on our finances. It is a direct representation of the choices we have made. Balance is the key. When you are very hungry and eat just enough to satisfy the body, you feel wonderful, almost euphoric. If you stuff yourself to the point of gluttony, you're going to feel quite sick. Life is very much like this. We need a balanced mix or we will never be able to enjoy our life to the fullest. So, as much as money is talked about in this book, it is not the real bottom line. It is about satisfying the body, soul and spirit, prioritizing our wants and needs and making appropriate choices. With a little planning and self-examination, you can learn about yourself and which choices are going to provide the most positive impact on your life. Hear is an acronym to help you remember what is involved in making the proper choices for you. C.H.O.I.C.E. is a Conscious, Healthy, Open-Minded, Intuitive, Creative and Educated decision.

One of my missions is to shed some light on the dynamics of the elusive, almighty dollar. What makes the dollar seem so mystical is that it can be very uncooperative. Have you discovered that money never seems to do what you want it to? As soon as little cash is directed toward a particular goal…Hello! Arriving quickly on the scene is a small disaster or crisis that needs the immediate attention of your funds. Sadly, the money that lands regularly in our accounts slips and slides it's way out of our hands. Poof! One minute it's here, the next it's gone. It doesn't take a rocket scientist to figure out that in order to save money, you've either got to spend less or make more. Unfortunately, those that make more, spend more. Therefore the debt to cash ratio stays the same, barely enough to make ends meet. Too frequently, we are left with too much month at the end of the money.

Our people and communities hold a wealth of knowledge and a rich culture and tradition that we have drifted away from. By getting back to those basics we can lift each other up. There are good, even great things going on in our neighborhoods every day. We can celebrate daily accomplishments, instead of wasting precious energy rallying against negative issues. Let's share good news, positive resources and bring victory to our lives. Ask any successful person you know how they got where they are today. If they're honest, they'll tell you that they didn't do it alone. Everyone needs a hand along the way. There is no shame in that.

I'm a born do-it-yourself-er. It's in my nature to test different uses for common items and new reasons for trying them. Ever since I was a young girl, our home bathroom and kitchen was my laboratory for concocting potions and dreaming up new ways to use common household goods. I would pour over magazines and books and try to duplicate products and designs for a fraction of the cost. Friends and relatives would ask how the heck my hair looked so good without a visit to the salon. Or how I could afford the clothes I wore on baby-sitting money. Years later, after moving into my own place, I found I could stretch my pitiful paycheck to afford a decent apartment, a dependable car, groceries in the fridge and still have money left to party! A few buddies suspected I had a secret sugar daddy, and it was about that time I realized my thrifty ways were like money in the bank! No one would believe me when I confessed to furnishing my place with other folk's throw-a-ways. I'll admit, after sprucing up this and that with paint and covering things with fabric, my crib was pretty fly. My standards are high, so I'm not talking "just making do". Those that followed my lead found they too could enjoy the good life without breaking their budget. My own sister dubbed me "Thrifty Sister" many years ago, and others whom I have helped have urged me to share my secrets.

There is an old saying that style is no substitute for substance. Substance is the quality of life that fulfills our soul. It is when we feel complete. A fullness that makes you feel whole and content. A life with dignity, peace and enjoyment. Loving, giving of yourself, caring, bettering your surroundings, spiritual connections and commitments; this is the stuff that makes life good. It fills a need deep in our soul, because it is the way God made us.

The African in America came to this country with nothing but memories of the homeland, their skills, strong-willed bodies and minds. We had courage, strength, intelligence and an intense desire to survive. Throughout the years, the African-American have proven to be a hardy, creative and resourceful people who thrived and flourished against all odds. We've created a wonderful cuisine based almost totally on food that was thrown away or deemed inedible by the slave owners.

Industrial growth and this country's prosperity were fueled by the back-breaking labor of the slave man and woman. Many modern day technologies and medical breakthroughs are based on inventions and the ingenuity of Black folks (though we didn't get the credit). Deprived of our cultural heritage and family ties, we fought hard to remember our roots. In order to fully dominate us, we were systematically brainwashed and brutalized. Our bodies, minds and lineage were ridiculed, de-humanized, abused and stripped away into an object of self-hate. Without ego or esteem, we turned on one another and ourselves.

Our history has shaped a multitude of internal thought patterns and personal habits that sometimes confuse us. We all have family traditions and cultural traits that have been passed down from generation to generation. This valuable contribution left to us by our ancestors can help us today. Remembering our past can help us step proudly into the future. We are royal heirs of kings and queens. Many of our genetic gifts motivate the types of food we like, the way we dress, wear our hair and the types of products we buy.

Some argue that integration was a detriment to Black society. After slavery, segregation was not totally negative. It had a positive side in that it produced Black professionals and businesses that served their own people. The carrot of "inclusion" with Whites encouraged us to abandon our own communities. It also set us up to go into direct competition with Whites for the similar jobs and housing areas. The job market grew thinner as automation eliminated jobs. Though integration was deemed law, racial discrimination was practiced daily as the unwritten law. Now men were struggling to support their families. What was left of the Black man's dignity and ego was crushed. As the family unit fell further apart, urban neighborhoods deteriorated. Some of the folks who prospered went on a journey of serving the "me" instead of the "we", and left their past behind.

The oppression we have suffered through slavery and racial discrimination have steered us toward products with short-term rewards like cars, clothes (including the dreaded dry-cleaning bill), lotto tickets, alcoholic beverages, hair and nail care products and services. Look around and see how many of these businesses are in your neighborhood. How many other types of commerce have taken up residence in your community? Some of these trends reflect back to the days when these type products represented the few options available for sale to the general Black community. We were shut out of any areas that promoted self-worth or income building, like high-paying jobs, property ownership and business investments.

Some folks still consider owning an automobile as "having made it". Great, you bought a car, but I shudder when I see a shiny, new car sitting in front of a shack. You can be proud to own a car, but don't stop there. Remember a car's worth diminishes as soon as you drive it off the lot. A car is an asset, which means it has value as long as you own it. Most of us are making payments on our car while it's in good condition. When you can no longer use it, it's not worth much. It does not gain equity, so it's not considered an investment. That's why unless you earn a large salary or are independently wealthy, spending an exorbitant amount on an expensive car is not wise. Where is the prestige if it gets repossessed and you're back to walking within a few months? Don't set yourself up to fail, stay within your means. A car is usually a necessity of life in order for you to get around, to work or even to do your work. Hopefully, by the end of this book, you will understand how much more you can achieve. I know you see plenty crumbling buildings with expensive cars parked up and down the block. Don't think they only belong to thugs and drug dealers. Hard working folks of today can still harbor the same negative, limited thinking that seemed to be a necessary evil of mental sanity and survival in the past.

We need all the personal and financial affirmation we can get. As an African-American woman, I see the frustration and hopelessness in the eyes of my sisters and brothers as their psyche is challenged on a daily basis. From the cradle, we've been told all the things we can't do. Unfortunately, these statements don't always come from other races. Self-hate and jealousy are rampant within our own backyards. Decide for yourself where you fit into life's puzzle. Search out your motives and reactions during various circumstances that occur in your own circle of friends and family. Are you a master builder or a demolition expert? Are you happy when others succeed or do you become secretly spiteful and vindictive? It's never to late to make self-discoveries and seek positive changes within your own persona. Spiritual and emotional growth should continue throughout our lives until the grave. Surround yourself with positive, nurturing people. Adding your own success to the community pot enriches others around you. Don't believe that one person can't make difference. Your contribution does matter. Negative energy drains the body. A negative attitude defeats the spirit, and can become a self-fulfilling prophecy. Think poor and you will be poor.

Do you know someone who can't seem to hold on to money? Someone who gets a bit of cash every now and then, but before they've barely got time to get the bills greasy, that money has vanished. In no time they are right back in the same financial bind, no closer to a better future. When asked what happened, they most likely won't know or perhaps don't want to tell. Hear me now; I'm talking about working folk, not the unemployed! The very next week, that same person will be complaining about how hard their life is and how they can't make ends meet. This type personality deals with life in a haphazard fashion, wheeling and dealing without any vision or foresight of the future. Without a plan in place, extra cash gets spent randomly and carelessly. And wouldn't you know it, here comes that unexpected bill or crisis, and there they are, tapped out of funds and playing the victim.

Money can throw us into a web of confusion, if we use finances as a gauge for a satisfied life. Without cash we experience any or some of the following emotions; frustration, anger, sadness and hopelessness. We feel powerless in our circumstance and want to throw up our hands in despair. We can become resentful, complaining how we don't make enough or have as much money as we deserve. We tell ourselves that if we had more money, everything in our lives would be better.

Think about that weekly change that slips through your fingers; the small amounts we piddle away on a daily basis. If you kept a record of all those "minor" purchases, they would add up to more cash than you ever imagined. With more cash accumulated, you can "afford" the types of major purchases you thought were out of your league. That feeling of satisfaction of achieving your goal, no matter how small, is empowerment to managing your piece of the world. We literally throw money away when we don't have a plan for our future.

Let me tell you about my co-worker, Coreen. She comes into work each day dressed to kill. Shoes matching the bag matching the outfit. Nails are perfect, hair from who knows where. We speak, but I noticed she gets a bit quiet when I come around. I overheard her tell some colleagues that I think I'm cute. (Fast rewind to high school.) From our first meeting, I thought I was snubbed because of my lack of interest in fashion. I dress quite plain unless it is for a special occasion and prefer sneakers to heels. On the flip side, I drive a nice ride, own my condo, my nails, hair and teeth are my own and I'm not bad to look at. As time passed, her ice slowly melted. Finally, I realized what her initial problem was. She was jealous of me. After getting to know her, I realized her exterior appearance was hiding the fact she was deep in debt, riding the bus or begging a ride.

As we were window-shopping during our lunch break one day, we passed an upscale furniture store. Coreen spied a couch and instantly fell in love with it. The couch was a high-quality piece, well made with beautiful fabric. She began to think in her old "poor mentality", and quickly put the possibility of owning the couch out of her mind. (We can mentally take ourselves out of the race before we've even tried to run it.) I watched her face change from joy to defeat as she gave in to her own self-limiting, mental dialogue. As we walked to my car, I began to tell her I accumulated the down payment for my car by saving my lunch money. She didn't believe it, but I could tell I had piqued her interest. We sat down the very next week and overhauled her budget. She was astonished at how much money was actually available, if she made some small changes in her spending habits. First, she had to evaluate what was really important in her life. She had to prioritize which habits were necessary and which were expendable. Or at least alterable. For instance, she could still get here nails done. Maybe not her usual once a week, but two times a month. She could eliminate the fancy jewels, color and designs she had added to the nails. She already had enough clothes to last a good, long time, but it was time for her to do some self-examination. Why did she feel the need to buy so many expensive clothes? After some thought she came to the conclusion that she shopped to feel better about her living conditions. It wasn't that she really needed the clothes. We discussed the irony of her discovery. She as doing the very thing that was stopping her from improving the situation she was depressed about! Once she understood her motives, she *wanted* to take steps to change her ways. She decided to cut her shopping trips from once a week to once a month and with a set amount to spend. The whole endeavor became a life-changing experience. This was no longer just about a couch; she was gaining insight about herself. Her successful investment boosted her confidence in her ability to manage her income. Her value system began to shift. In a short time, without an extra dime coming in, her standard of living improved.

Use this book as a guide to help you develop your own thrifty style. It's up to you how thrifty you want to be. It all depends on your own personal needs and what you wish to accomplish. The great thing about thrift is it's not an exact science—strike your own balance—feel free to modify! Take my hand and see how quickly you will identify with the thrifty lifestyle. Many of the tips in this book have been gathered over many years. Some are of my own invention and experiences, while others have been shared or passed from one to another. You won't be doing without; you'll just be doing things differently. This is why you won't feel deprived, poor or cheap. You'll be astounded how flexible your lifestyle can be. When you get thrifty, you're in control. This new way of thinking will allow you to become a creative problem solver. You will gain a new found freedom with your finances that feels downright good. Your options will increase and your hard-earned money will work harder for you. Isn't that better than being a slave to your budget?

I know that gifts, (especially gifts from God) are not gifts unless they are shared. So...those of you that are tired of spinning your wheels and getting nowhere, prepare for your own personal success with Thrifty Sister!

Chapter 2: Thrifty Concepts

Can we start by first agreeing that we all have some blessings to count? Anyone reading this page right now has life, eyesight and enough education to read these lines! A positive approach to life's challenges is half the battle. Think about all the things in your life to be thankful for. Many of them have nothing to do with money. Most of us take for granted the basics like good health, shelter (no matter how humble), food and a few friends. Think of those living in a third world country or back in the day when people were not free to make their own choices in life. We have a lot of things going for us in this country, whether we want to admit or not. It's important to remember to appreciate and take care of what we have right now. It will be good practice for the abundant life we expect to have. If you don't value where and what you have today, how will you manage more? What will you do with those blessings received later? Could that be a factor in why you are struggling today? Learning to take care of our current assets in a way that will make them function more efficiently and last longer means more time will pass before we have to dig in our pockets and replace them. Isn't it wonderful that just by keeping what you own longer can raise your living standard?

It's time to get on board with an action plan that will bring life-changing results. Webster's dictionary breaks down the word "thrifty" this way: "*Thriving by industry and frugality. Growing vigorously. Practicing economy and good management. Provident.*" Translation meaning we can become prosperous by incorporating thrifty habits into our daily routine. The most basic and useful thrifty habit to acquire is the ability to take the best care possible of what we are already blessed with. This includes all areas of our lives; body, spirit, soul, goals, dreams, loved ones and material possessions.

Adapting a "can-do" attitude, while visualizing yourself where you want to be, can make your quest for financial stability an uplifting journey. The way we handle our possessions is a direct reflection of how we feel about ourselves. Let your imagination run free as you consider all the possibilities you'd like to experience in the future.

I happen to love the thrifty lifestyle. It allows me to splurge on the things that I really love. No, that's not a contradiction, even though the two words, "thrifty" and "splurge" seem to be opposites. In actuality, these two actions actually compliment one another. Without darkness there is no light. Similarly, living thrifty with regards to basic goods and services allows me the luxury of deciding how the savings will be spent.

With that said, walk with me as we take some fundamental steps to creating your own personal style of thrifty living. Take the time to read and complete each step as thoroughly as possible. Each step will enlighten and empower you and is designed to help you discover your basic tendencies and practices. They'll provide you with insight on how, why and when you spend, and how some of these habits may be sabotaging your goals. You can then put together your own action plan that will be customized to your individuality.

STEP 1—*Examine Your Current Budget*

Make a list of your monthly budget using the following form:

MONTHLY EXPENSES	AMOUNT
NET MONTHLY INCOME (take home)	
1. Rent / Mortgage	
2. Utilities (Electric / Gas / Water)	
3. Phone Bill	
4. Total Credit Cards (Minimum Payments)	
5. Transportation or Car Payment	
6. Gas (1 week x 4)	
7. Clothes (monthly average)	
8. Insurance (Car, Home)	
9. Groceries (1 week x 4)	
10. Family (Sports/Hobbies/Allowance)	
11. Misc. Spending Money (1 week x 4)**	
12. Entertainment (Movies, Dinner)	
13. Charitable Contributions (Yes, you can!)	
TOTAL EXPENSES Add Lines 1—13	
BALANCE	

Add lines number one through 13. Subtract this amount from your Net Monthly Income and record your balance. This is the first step in your journey to self-reliance and awareness. Your balance is yourstarting point. Your total expenses should not exceed your monthly income. If they do, don't despair. There is hope, no matter what your situation, just keep reading!

STEP 2—*Identify Problem Areas & Eliminate Waste*

Waste is a bad habit, whether you can afford it or not. If you're living from paycheck to paycheck, waste is deadly. The American media culture bombards us with ads that dictate what and how much we need. According to them, we need everything, and we need it today! We buy groceries that don't get eaten, clothes we don't wear (OK, maybe once!), jewelry we don't need, and a multitude of miscellaneous items we could surely live without. Wasteful habits are insidious, too. They sneak into our lifestyle and develop into habits without our detecting their presence. After all, everyone else is doing it!

Identify your worst, wasteful habits and begin to take steps to change your ways. Recalling the numbers you recorded in the previous chart, identify your monthly money nightmares. Does the room start to spin when you open your phone bill? Is your light bill going through the roof? Do you forget to turn off lights or keep the TV running all day? Do you have your heat turned way up or the air conditioner way down? How many department store charge cards do you have? Are you still paying for items you no longer use? What is the interest rate on those charge cards? Do you spend money on clothes that you really don't need? (You probably still say you have nothing to wear.) Do you make phone calls whenever you feel like it, or when rates are cheaper? Are you beginning to see how many areas can affect your monthly budget? Simple habitual changes can save you big right away.

STEP 3—*Find Your Spending Style*

Identify your spending style. Make a list of when and what nonessential purchases you make. This does not include your monthly bills. I'm talking about those black holes in time where your daily or weekly allotment magically disappears. Chances are you'll have to think hard to remember where it went. Impulse buying gives us a short burst of satisfaction that quickly changes to guilt and empty pockets. When the paycheck runs out, you become frustrated that you're broke. Your frustration can turn into aggravation, depression or anger as you try to place blame on something or someone. These negative emotions only make us feel even more out of control.

Most folks are shocked when they discover how much money is actually being spent on what we consider small incidentals. With advertisements constantly yapping in our ears about what we need, it's easy to get caught picking up little things here and there. However, when it's time to do something that is important to you, but unaffordable at the time, we feel deprived and discouraged, like we just can't get ahead. That's because without a goal, saving money has no real meaning. Major purchases like dream homes, vacations and cars seem totally out of reach.

Are you an emotional binge spender? Do you buy things when you're angry or depressed? During these times it's easy to convince yourself that you work hard, you deserve the best and blah, blah, blah. This is a dangerous cycle because each time you get frustrated about your finances, you go deeper in debt.

For the next week or two (or however long it takes to go from one paycheck to another), write down every item you purchase along with the price. Be totally honest and carry a pad with you at all times so you don't miss even one purchase. Don't try to fool yourself by changing your spending habits. Just keep a close record of all your usual spending activity. This is going to be a real eye opener. Until you understand exactly what you're battling against, you won't be able to win the war.

Once you've recorded your activity, look over the numbers. Are you surprised at the total amount? If so, how important were any of those purchases and how many could you have done without? Go back and look at item number 11 on your expense chart (page 13). Compare and record your new entry. How does this change your bottom line?

STEP 4—*Make a Goals List*

The desires of your heart don't have to be elaborate, but they are important. They are, after all, your own personal needs. We all want, need and dream differently. The trap can be not recognizing the important difference between goals and dreams. A dream is usually something you don't believe you can achieve. You watch movie and music stars on television and wish you were them. You envy others possessions without ever planning on putting in the blood, sweat and tears to achieve what they have. Dreams are wishes that float around in an ethereal cloud, bouncing off the sides of our cranial lobes. They serve no real purpose nor involve any concrete activity other than wasting precious time. Some people actually begin to feel a sense of accomplishment just by obsessively thinking about their passion. Have you ever thought about doing something so much that you fooled yourself into believing that you actually did it?

Alternatively, goals are dreams with a time-line and action plan. Without those two elements in place, your desires will never pass the dream stage. Forming a thrifty action plan can change your wishes into active aspirations.

Do you fantasize about home ownership, vacationing on an exotic island or buying a new car? Do you have kids that you intend to send to college, or maybe you'd like to send yourself? Perhaps you'd just like to afford dinner out once a month, join a gym or learn a new hobby. Begin your list with mini goals and build to the larger ones. Start with your most simple ambitions you believe you can achieve fairly easily and work your way to a full-blown fantasy. Don't be afraid to shoot for the moon. Remember, this is all still on paper. Now break down the largest goals into smaller, more manageable goals that will serve to keep you on course, all the way to the finish line.

For example, the big goal may be to buy a brand new car. Once you have identified your goal, you will need to become an informed consumer on the subject matter. Don't rely on salesmen and relatives to give you information. Get yourself a little notebook and give it an appropriate label (like That Damn Car I Intend To Buy). Become an investigative reporter for your acquisition. The Internet is a great place to search out information. If not, make phone calls to at least three dealerships and compare prices. Find out if any rebates or specials are running. Ask about yearly promotional times, like fall inventory or wintertime buying slumps. Go to the library for consumer reports on the car of your choice and make sure it's a good purchase for you. Who knows, you may have had your heart set on a two-seater, but you have three kids! Or you love the big SUV's, but drive 50 miles each way to work. You won't be able to afford the gas, never mind the car payment. The objective is to make sound decisions and purchases that will satisfy and serve your needs for a good, long time. There is nothing worse than spending your hard earned cash without being confident that you got the best buy. Believe me, there are so many choices; you will find the right fit for you. Write down the things you absolutely must have in a car (like air-conditioning or automatic transmission); then the features that you could do without (like a CD player, or power windows). The trick is to not get too romantic about your purchase. You don't have to give up style or comfort, but be ready to compromise. Armed with knowledge and a little patience, you'll find exactly what you're looking for and spend the amount you intended.

Ok. You have calculated that by saving $3000 for a down payment will leave a manageable monthly car payment that fits your budget. The next step is to figure out how long it will take you to save up that amount (using the tips in this book, of course!). You would have to save $250.00 per month to save up the money in one year. See Chapter 3: Shop Talk and find out how you can quickly and painlessly save at least $25 per week from your grocery bill. Add a mini goal of saving an additional $10 per week toward your car fund. (This can be done as easily as bringing instant coffee to work rather than buying it!) Guess what, you've already realized half your goal! By the time you have saved your down payment, you'll have disciplined yourself enough to never miss a car note, once you're behind the drivers seat! Reward yourself with a non-monetary treat each time your reach your monthly goal. Focus on the mini successes to keep yourself motivated to stay the course of the larger goal without getting discouraged.

STEP 5—*Prioritize Your Spending Options*

At this point your eyes are wide open about where your money is going and why. You also have your goals list. Take into consideration where your future purchases fit into your personal vision for your future. Remember, I said that a thrifty lifestyle doesn't have to be painful, so it's wise to be honest about what you can and can't do without. If you're not sure (that's okay, you're new at this), here are some guidelines that may help you decide on what stays and what goes.

Consider this equation: Need + Benefits vs. Life Span + Cost.

Need: How bad do you really need this item? How long can you do without it? Is being without it a daily source of conflict and aggravation, or do you only think of it occasionally? Maybe you only think about it when someone brings it up or you see someone else with it.

Benefit: What is purchasing this item doing to do for you? Is it a stepping-stone to more income or will it be a drain on your budget. How much do you intend to use this purchase? Daily, weekly, monthly, or rarely? How long will you be satisfied with this item?

Life Span: How long do you intend for this item to last vs. the manufacturer's life span? Are those numbers close? Write down the number between 1 and 20 years.

Cost: How affordable is this item and what effects will it have on your monthly budget? Is this the model you love or are you settling for less because of the price? Have you comparison shopped and found out what the market value is? Will this item depreciate or increase in value over time? How long will it take you to pay it off, or can you pay for it outright?

Here's an example. Your annual office Christmas party is in two weeks. You saw this wonderful outfit that you fell in love with and will really set you apart from the crowd. Consider one side of the equation: Need + Benefit. Do you really need this outfit or do you have something else in your closet that will look nice? Will there be some networking opportunities at this party? Will this outfit bring you a raise or snare you a husband? What benefits will this item bring you, and why do you feel so desperate to have it? Could you be trying to fill an unrelated void in your life?

Now for the other side: *Life span + Cost*. How long to you intend to get use from this outfit? Will you wear it often or rarely? How much will you have to pay to have it cleaned? Will the price tag set you back or do you have a few dollars saved for such a purchase? Is there something else you'll have to do without in order to afford the outfit? If so, how is that going to make you feel later?

This may seem like a lot to go through before we buy something if you're not used to it. For me it's second nature to quickly sift through the reasoning quickly, and you will too with a little practice. If you think about it, it's really sad that we don't seriously evaluate each and every item we purchase. The American mentality of gluttony and capitalistic cannibalism has ruined many a family. Please, don't buy into the media propaganda that your possessions define who you are.

Step 6—Apply Smart Money Practices

Pay Off High Interest Credit Cards. Look over your statements and see how much interest you pay monthly versus the return on a savings account. Credit cards can cost you up to 23% monthly. Savings accounts only return 1-3%. The quicker you get that loan paid off, the more money you will save.

Pay Your Bills First. This is a habit I've had ever since I supported myself. Actually that's not true. My parents were very instrumental in fostering this trait in their children. They did it by making me honor my commitments at home. If I borrowed money from my Dad, he expected to be paid back. He didn't forget about it, and you best believe I didn't get anything else until it was paid. These were powerful lessons (not that I thought it at the time), and prepared me for the real worlds' unsympathetic ways.

Bills don't go away because you pretend they aren't there. Leave them unopened and they just pile up, ruining your credit. Once your financial condition gets out of hand, it's very hard to get them back in control. It can cost you time, money, stress and embarrassment. Nasty bill collectors hound you at home and work. Devise a bill-paying system that you can stick to. I use a wicker mail holder with three tiers to organize my bills in a conspicuous place. The top compartment holds current bill info that I may need to refer to later, like recently paid off statements that reflect the zero balance. This is a handy reference of my account number, balance payoff amounts and dates. (Credit companies are notorious for adding some latent charge after an account has been paid off or closed, like membership fees or finance penalties.) The second tier is where I store incoming bills pending payment. They are opened immediately, where the amount and due date are calculated. Bills that are due in the current week are moved down into the first tier for payment. Stamps and return address stickers are kept in the first tier also. Some people keep a calendar and write their due dates on their planner. Find a safe place and devise a monthly plan for getting your bills out on time. The company should receive your payments by the due date, not mailed out on that date. If you are mailing out on the due date, your payments will always be late. Once you've paid your bills you can make decisions on where the rest, if any, will be spent. Your spending money is a variable, either its there or it isn't. There's an old saying that there is never enough money to get what you need, but you can always find money to buy what you want. When your bills are paid first, however you decide to spend the rest won't have as big of an impact on your overall budget.

Good Credit Pays Off. When it's time to buy those big-ticket items like a car or house, good credit becomes a critical factor. Most people can't afford to pay cash for the full amount, so you're going to need a loan. Your bill-paying history can bless you or haunt you. Now I know you know we Black folks already have a hard time getting loans. Don't add bad credit to the mix! Remember, you want to be in control and make your own decisions. A good credit history gives you leverage and bargaining power. Those who deal in dollars want to loan to a good credit risk, it's how they make their money. Don't wind up at the mercy of some financial institution who will charge you loan-shark rates because you're a bad credit risk, or turned down flat all together. Having good credit translates into qualifying for low-interest credit cards and lower insurance rates. Did you know if you have a good track record of paying your utilities, telephone or cable bill, they would waive any security deposits? In this day of high-technology and access to all types of records, your credit affects whether or not you may be approved to even rent an apartment! Employers are now screening potential employees by checking their credit history. They realize these records tell a lot about a person's character and whether or not they are dependable. If you're credits not good now, take out a small loan, pay it back on time and start to rebuild your credit history.

Learn How to Complain. You're celebrating a joyous occasion and have planned a special night out. You feel good cause you're treating your loved ones to a special meal with cash you saved. To your dismay, the waiter is preoccupied, ignoring your party most of the night and the food is cold and tasteless. You don't want to further ruin the evening so you keep silent, swearing to never frequent that restaurant again. Before you ban the joint, try complaining effectively.

How many products and services have you paid for that were faulty or unsatisfactory? Most people don't bother, feel helpless or say they don't have the time or energy to complain. I don't know about you, but my money and my time are too precious to squander. Remember, if what you bought isn't working, you're going to have to replace it. That means you're paying twice for the same product. The Better Business Bureau reports that 25% of purchases or services result in loss, yet only 1 in 25 complain! You can best believe that companies depend on this percentage…it's why many of them don't bother to clean up their act.

The good news is that by learning how to effectively complain, you can recoup your losses. Some companies really care about customer satisfaction and will compensate you for your troubles. This can come in the form of free meals, upgrades, vouchers, free tickets or replacing the item altogether. Standing up for yourself bolsters your self-esteem. Demanding your respect and self-express is a powerful tool that will help you in other areas of your life. It definitely pays to complain, and getting what you paid for is your right as a consumer. Here's how:

1. Get your facts in order. Gather all pertinent receipts, warranties and any relevant paperwork.

2. Call the company. Be prepared to state the problem in a comprehensive manner without cursing or a nasty attitude. Yelling at people will get you nowhere fast. Ask to be referred to a manager, supervisor or owner if the person speaking to can't seem to help you. Write down names and phone numbers of all the people you speak to, and take notes of the conversation.

3. If you don't get satisfaction with the call, write the company. Address your letter to the president or owner of the establishment. Again, word your letter so that it's short and too the point without

any name calling. Make sure the letter is typed or printed legibly. Include your name, address and phone number so they can get in touch with you. At the end of the letter, carbon copy the Better Business Bureau (check the yellow pages for the branch nearest you), and send them a copy.

4. Still no satisfaction? File a complaint by calling the Better Business Bureau and refer to the letter that was sent earlier. They report that 50% of all filed complaints get resolved satisfactorily without their intervention.

Quality vs. Quantity. We thrifty people know that price is not the only consideration when making purchases, especially big-ticket items like furniture or appliances. Because you expect these items to last you a long time, buying cheap is not a good idea. Spending $200 on an item that will last 2 years versus paying $400 for an item that will last 10 years will cost you more than the $200 difference later on. Replacement value of that same item 2 years later will cost you more than $200. Don't forget you'll have to dispose of the old item. Some cities charge to remove large appliances and furniture. And who wants to have to come up with another chunk of cash so soon? So now, 4 years have gone and you've spent $500 for an item that's destined to die in another 2 years. 6 years later you've spent an additional $300 to replace that same item, so now you've spent $800 and so on. Can you see that paying $400 for a quality item up front has actually saved you money? You want to be able to make a quality purchase that you won't have to worry about replacing anytime soon. This allows you to move forward rather than in circles. Shop around; ask friends and family about products they recommend. Bide your time, watch sales and sock some money away while you wait. When the one you want is in your reach…GRAB IT. Strike a balance between the two features of price and quality merchandise. You'll be much happier with your decision many years down the road.

Chapter 3: Shop Talk

Which is it, the rising cost of food or your family's rising appetites that's got your down? Wouldn't you like to leave the market happy instead of dazed? You scrutinize the register tape, wondering how the heck you spent so much more than you intended. This weekly quest to stay within your budget can be a well of opportunity. Not only can you stay within your budget, you can greatly reduce it!

Your grocery allotment can be a valuable source of extra cash flow. Monthly bills like your rent, mortgage or car payment are set amounts and can't be adjusted just because your paycheck is short. Do that often enough and you'll be out on the street or taking the bus. However, your food bill is a variable expense. No one can force you to pay a certain amount on groceries each week. What happens is we fall into the habit of making the same type purchases each week, whether we have planned to use them or not. I'll bet there is enough food in your cabinets and refrigerator right now to sustain the household for at least a week or two. That's if you really had to.

Perhaps you feel that you're running to the grocery store way too often. As soon as you return with one item, you run out of another, right? It can be very frustrating trying to bring home the bacon, and still have enough bacon left to fry!

Having the option to decide what and when you'll spend allows for financial freedom that feels downright good. Some time ago, while fixing dinner, I realized I was out of my usual bottled spaghetti sauce. Rather than dropping everything and dashing to the store, I checked the kitchen.

I found two tomatoes, a piece of onion and a can of tomato sauce. I threw it together and added some seasoning and whalla! Homemade spaghetti sauce. It felt good getting over and even my man was impressed. Plus, the sauce actually tasted better than the jar brand. Follow my lead and watch the shock on your family's face when you bring sirloin to the table instead of hot dogs. Create a great meal when there's nothing (to the untrained eye) in the fridge.

Pick and choose the ideas that work with your lifestyle. I guarantee that you can chop at least 25% off your total weekly grocery bill. In real numbers, this means even if you only shave off $5 per week, you've saved $20 a month. This can be as easy as eliminating two items off your grocery list. (I'm sure you can think of at least two things you could have done without!) Put some real thought into streamlining your purchases, and you can cut back by a whopping 50%! Hey, what you do with the extra money is your business. Don't worry, I'm not going to tell you to get on line for "gov'ment cheese" or have bread and water for breakfast. I won't advise you to shop at five different stores to grab a special from each one. Once you add in time and gas spent plus the aggravation factor, you haven't saved a bit. This thrifty sister doesn't believe in sacrificing a decent quality of life in the name of saving a buck.

The suggestions ahead can be tried and tested immediately. They are quick and easy to do. Through them, you'll become a savvy consumer, wise in the ways of advertising ploys. This will enable you to make healthy, cost-cutting choices in what and how you buy. All you need is an adventurous spirit, a little knowledge and the desire to save.

The common goal is to reduce the amount you spend in any given month. Doing this will leave you with leftover money (is there such a thing?) that you can divert towards the lifestyle you've always wanted. Keeping your focus on small, manageable goals will help you stick to your plan. This way, if you blow it one week, you can make it up during the next week. Don't give up on the war just because you lose a couple of battles. Keep the big picture in mind and decide right now that you're in it for the long haul. You are in control when you plan your strategy. It's up to you to decide how severely you need to cut back. For me, thrift doesn't represent cutting back, it is redirecting the cash flow to satisfy rather than just survive. Make up your mind that you won't fall totally off the wagon just because of one setback. Get right back on that horse and ride!!

The Grocery List

Improving your odds of lowering your food bill while still eating a well-balanced diet begins with a well-planned shopping list. Remember, you've only got two ways to increase your earning power, make more money or spend less.

My motto is "use what you buy and buy only what you need". What we like to eat often stems from our upbringing. When we strike out on our own, we tend to shop the same way our parents did. There's nothing wrong with tradition, but don't get trapped into buying items just because it was your mother's favorite, or it's comforting seeing it in the fridge (until it's rotten and you have to toss it).

One day I realized I was buying one green pepper every week. And every other week I was throwing out one green pepper. I just bought it out of habit. Sure, I thought I was going to use it for something, but then I never did. Now I only buy peppers when I have planned a meal that requires it. Maybe your family's tastes have changed and there are foods you buy that nobody eats anymore.

Plan Your Meals

Go through your refrigerator and cabinets and check out what's there. Take note of their condition and make a mental note of how long they've been there and why. Are there any fresh fruits and veggies you should have consumed or not bought at all? What you want to do is use up any perishables that are edible and throw out the rotten stuff. Plan meals that include those ingredients first. Check out the freezer and look over your frozen items. If there is unrecognizable food in it, open them up, use them or toss them out. You want to make a fresh start. Unless you are only cooking for yourself, try not to make too many drastic changes at first. You don't want mutiny in the household the first week out. Balance is the name of the thrifty game. It's not supposed to be painful.

Plan menus for the number of days till your next shopping trip. Try to work in at least one meatless meal per week. Small, slow shifts in the way you think about food encourages change in habits that were sabotaging your goals.

Write Your List

Now it's time to sit down with your favorite supermarket circular. Mine is from the store that provides me the most savings when I do my biggest shopping. I do occasionally travel to another market nearby that has a few great specials, but I'm careful to buy only what I came for. On those trips, I sometimes check out the prices of items I normally buy, just to see the difference. (Only do this if you are disciplined enough to resist impulse buying.) Write down or keep a mental record of prices. You'll get a feel for which supermarket gives you the products you want at the best price.

Go through the circular with your meal plan handy. Write a list that includes the ingredients that fit into your meal plan. There's still plenty of time to be flexible. If you see an item at a great price, plan on buying more than one and/or making extra meals for freezing. Make sure to check out fresh fruits and vegetables in season and on sale.

Once you get acclimated to the market of your choice, you'll be able to visualize the aisle layout (i.e., cereals on aisle 1, health & beauty on aisle 2, etc.) of the supermarket as your write your list. Order your list according to the pattern you shop in. For example, if you start on the outer aisles, write those items first on the list. If you don't have it memorized, jot down the aisle layout next time you shop. By doing this, you have less chance of skipping items on your list as you shop. You don't want to have to back-track to pick up forgotten items.

Heading to the market with an accurate list shortens the length of time spent in the store. You'll also cut down on impulse buying (purchasing unnecessary items on the spur of the moment) that often occurs on those side-trips hunting for a missed item. One survey stated that every extra five minutes spent in the store adds an average of $10 to the total bill. That's a scary concept, so you want to get in and out in a hurry, and keep those blinders on while you shop. Stick to your list. On weeks when I'm on the bare bones plan, I calculate the cost of each item and make sure my total is within my budget before I hit the register. If you need to, carry a small calculator and keep a running tally as you add items to your cart.

Healthier and Cheaper

It's a common misconception that eating healthier costs more. Most people think that altering the way they eat, shop and cook is going to cost them a bundle. Truth is, you can eat healthier and spend less. I've spent years in supermarkets observing other people's carts and what they have in them. I've noticed Black folks often buy processed foods and canned goods. When I ask why, the answer is they think it's cheaper. In reality, these products cost more per serving than making fresh, and can be harmful to our health.

Our history has shaped many of the foods we gravitate towards. The phrase "living high off the hog" goes back to slavery days. The slave owners would have hogs slaughtered and ate the leaner, tender meat from the upper body of the pig. The lower, undesirable cuts and the organs were left to the slaves. (Don't act like you don't know.... hog maws, hocks, ears, guts, etc.) A large portion of our diet consisted of salt, pork, corn and flour. Cornmeal was a staple and was the basis of many recipes. Stripped from our African homeland and our native foods, we had to create our own cuisine from the limited foodstuffs allowed us. What a hardy, creative people we are!

Still, the health statistics of African-Americans have historically been poor. On the average, Black people live six years less than other races in this country. Recent surveys have shown that the African-American diet is in dire need of healthy modifications. A recent Heart & Soul Food Marketing Institute Shopping for Health survey found that 42% of Blacks strongly believe that "it costs more to eat healthy foods". However, 58% felt strongly that nutrition is more important than price and 72% would be willing to pay more for healthier versions of the foods they normally eat. So it should be wonderful news to all that it is possible to buy smarter, healthier and still spend less.

How many friends and relative do you have that are plagued with high blood pressure, diabetes and heart problems? Truth be told, we can't afford NOT to eat right! We are already victims of daily stressful situations that are beyond our control. It's time to do something about the areas we can control, don't you agree?

Take note of the following healthy strategies that will cost less too.

- Do you really know what you're eating? Buying and consuming food closest to their natural state will save you money and improve your diet. When you know what ingredients go into your dishes, you can feel good about feeding it to your family. Why buy frozen French fries and spud flakes when all you need is a five or ten pound bag of potatoes? Prepared foods cost lots more and often contain additives you don't need like salt, sugar, preservatives and fat.

- Here's a simple visual to help you stay focused on the "good" foods. Shop the outer aisles of the supermarket. This is where fresh fruits, vegetables, meats, breads and dairy items reside. The inner aisles are stocked with less nutritious canned goods, sweets, packaged foods and mixes.

- Make traditional foods healthier by replacing fatty pork meat with smoked turkey. More and more of our folks are turning up their nose at pork, but you know they still love the flavor! Smoked turkey is meatier and leaner than neck bones and ham hocks, so you get more for your money. And have you checked out the prices they are charging for bony pork cuts and fat back? Don't let it be around holiday time when the price really jumps! It's a shame how these businesses can turn an item that used to be poor folks fodder into a gourmet priced food. I prefer turkey wings because in my opinion, turkey legs are a bit too lean and muscular to add a strong, rich flavor. Either way, any cut of smoked turkey is a tasty, healthy alternative to pork. Make up your own mind.

- Want pork flavor without the meat? Goya makes an inexpensive substitute—ham seasoning. These concentrated seasoning packets come 8 in a box for 99 cents, and do a great job of fooling your taste buds. They are meat-free (but do contain some MSG). There may be other brand names in your area and are definitely worth checking out.

- Don't forget the beans. They are still one of the most inexpensive, healthy ways to eat. A slow cooker is an easy, wonderful way to cook dried beans. You don't have to soak them overnight and are cheaper and healthier. Canned beans are OK, but cost more, have added salt and have been processed. Beans are an excellent source of protein and fiber. Explore all the imaginative ways to enjoy them.

- Canola oil is the healthiest and cheapest oil to use in cooking and for salad dressings. Making your own salad dressing is purer and cheaper. Add some vinegar and experiment with herbs and seasonings you have on hand.

- The price of spices can be outrageous. I don't know about you, but I'm so glad 99 cents spice lines have emerged. They offer almost any type of spice you can think of at a fraction of the cost. Use less salt in your cooking and substitute a variety of spices to compliment your food. Many a TV chef may advise you to use only the "good" spices, which I guess means high priced, gourmet seasonings. I've used the budget line since they came out and haven't had a complaint about my cooking yet. Matter of fact, nobody knows the difference.

- Make your own broth that is low in fat and salt by boiling the parts of meat that gets trimmed off, i.e., skin, fat, organs, etc. (Throw in some of those wilted veggies for extra flavor!) Strain the broth, refrigerate overnight (the fat will rise and harden on the top) and simply lift the "lid" of fat off. You can freeze the broth or refrigerate and use within one week.

- Eat heart healthy by using your homemade broth for sautéing and flavor instead of butter or margarine. Use the broth in place of the cooking water for flavorful rice, noodles or boiled potatoes. Keep handy broth "cubes" by freezing broth in a spare ice cube tray. Cover with plastic wrap. Pop out convenient sized cubes that go directly from the freezer into the pan.

- If you're trying to cut down on fat (and who isn't nowadays), fresh ground turkey is a great alternative to ground beef. Pound for pound, ground turkey cost less than the same fat percentage of beef. You'll wind up with more meat for your money that's better for you. It is not as heavy and is easier to digest. It absorbs more of the flavor of whatever you mix in it. Use it for spaghetti sauce, tacos, sloppy joes or meat loaf. Personally, I don't recommend it for plain burgers, the meat is a little too lean and can be tough. Ground turkey is cheapest when bought frozen. I recently paid a mere 50 cents a pound for ground turkey. Frozen, it looks like a roll of sausage. I mix this with ground beef for burgers or meat loaf, or any dish that isn't in a sauce. If you don't tell the family, I'll bet they won't notice the difference.

- Decide what is really the cheaper buy. Purchasing a cheap item that no one eats is a total waste of money. Foods with "no waste" value may actually cost you less in the long run. That's why I believe in occasionally buying boneless cuts of meat and poultry. Let's do the math. Come on! The thrifty mind doesn't resent a little work. The rewards are well worth the effort. You may think 69 cents a pound is a good price whole chicken. Most chickens average between 2 ½ to 4 lbs., so a 3-½ pound chicken costs about $2.50. Boneless chicken cutlets are regularly on sale for $1.99 a pound. You may think you can't afford that. Up front it seems that 69 cents per pound versus $1.99 is saving you big. But lets look at what you have actually bought. In an average whole chicken, you get 1 pound of bone, .7 lbs. of skin and ½ pound of organ meat. This adds up to 1-½ pounds of waste. You are left with 1 pound of boneless poultry and spent $2.50 for that pound. Take into account the time it takes to thaw, clean and cut up the chicken. In the end, you've spent 50 cents more per pound and added preparation time to the equation. That $1.99 you originally thought was high doesn't seem so unreasonable now, and all you have to do is unwrap it and get cooking.

- Eggs are still an inexpensive alternative to meat and it doesn't have to always be served for breakfast. New studies have blasted the cholesterol hype of the early '90's and proven that eggs, eaten in moderation do not significantly increase cholesterol levels.

- It's healthier and cheaper to cut back on the meat in your recipes. It's easy to do when you make casseroles, stews, stir-fry dishes and soups. A few examples of meatless dinners are linguini & clam sauce, spaghetti marinara, tuna casserole or even macaroni & cheese as the entrée. Check out a vegetarian cookbook for different ideas. Make It's only about 2 or 3 times a week now that I serve the traditional three dish meal with meat as the focus.

- Take advantage of fresh fruits and vegetables in season when they're cheapest and in the best condition. Buy extras of your favorites and freeze immediately in vacuum-sealed baggies. Best picks for fruits are grapes and sliced bananas (to be eaten frozen). Any type of berry and pineapple (crush or cube for best results), which can be eaten after thawing. They can also be frozen with sugar to use in deserts.

- Don't forget to visit your local farmer's market during the summer and fall months. Items sold here are generally cheaper and taste better because they are grown locally. You get fresh picked fruit and veggies that taste better than those bought at the supermarket. Another plus, growers from smaller farms tend to use fewer chemicals in their growing and harvesting process.

- Consider both the price and nutritional value of fresh food. Fresh produce in season is usually the healthiest and cheapest way to go. However, if it looks like it's been sitting on the shelf a bit too long, it's probably lost most of its vitamin content and good taste. In that case, frozen produce is a better buy because it gets process right after harvesting, sealing in the nutrients and flavor. Canned produce should be your last choice. Not only does canned foods contain added preservatives and salt, but also many of the nutrients have been destroyed by heat during the canning process.

- Reduce snack foods in your house in general. You pay a lot for a few chips or cookies that often get consumed in a mindless whirlwind. Snack foods are the source of more fat, salt and empty calories than any body needs. Better choice is to bake an occasional box cake, make cookies or even Jell-O.

Coupon Savvy

- Clip only the coupons for items you normally buy. It's doesn't pay to buy something simply for the sake of using a coupon (unless it's a free item). The only time to clip otherwise is it's for a new item you've wanted to try AND it's on sale.

- If you subscribe to any magazine or order products by mail, your name will be on a mailing list. The benefit of this is that you'll receive extra coupons, free samples and circulars in the mail. Okay, so you'll also get a bit more junk mail, but you can handle that, right? Buy your local newspaper on Wednesdays and/or Sundays to keep up with local happenings, sales and coupons and circulars.

- Many supermarkets have a coupon "swap box". This is basically a bin where customers dump and take coupons. Ask at the courtesy counter if they provide a box where customers can exchange their coupons. If they don't provide it, why not suggest starting one?

- Before you shop, place your coupons inside an envelope and write your list on the outside of the envelope.

- Find extra coupons along the grocery aisles in dispensers near the featured product.

- Take the time to get rain checks. Those hot sale items sell out quickly. Most stores will either offer brand exchanges or rain checks. These vouchers are good for at least a month or two, and some never expire. Its well worth the extra minutes it takes to go to the courtesy desk and request them. I've found rain checks to be especially handy on meat items. Seems like the cuts of meat get fattier when they are on sale. After the sale is over and the price goes up, use that rain check for leaner cuts of meat at the sale price!

- Take advantage of rebates, on-pack savings and coupons, and mail-in offers for products you use regularly.

- If you really want an expensive item, buy when it's on sale AND use a coupon. Use this concept for weekly items like cereal. Cereal manufacturers always offer coupons (I wonder why?). There are also some brands that have lowered their overall prices like Post.

- Coupons have gone digital. There are now web sites you can visit and subscribe to receive free coupons in the mail. It's reported that Americans clip more than 4.9 billion paper coupons per year. The queen of coupon distributors, Val-Pak joined other on-line bargain makers (www.valpak.com). Another major website for coupons is H.O.T.!Coupons.com. They offer more than 30,000 coupons for all types of services, including food, of course. You can even print your own coupons on-line straight to your printer. To use the service you must type in your zip code and pick a category. You'll get a list of coupons that can be printed out or used electronically. To view the whole gambit, simply use the search word "coupons" in your browser.

S-t-r-e-t-c-h Your Groceries

You've shopped, save money, done good. So good in fact, you're planning a little weekend getaway next month. Now that you've got the goods at home, here's how to make the most of what you bought.

- Get more yield by adding and extra cup of uncooked pasta, rice or two to three potatoes (leave the skin on for extra fiber and vitamins) to the side dish mixes like Potatoes au Gratin, Noodles & Sauce or Rice Medley's. Those packages don't make enough even to feed my family of four, however there is enough "sauce" to accommodate the extra bulk. You could also add fresh or frozen peas, broccoli or mixed vegetables and serve as a meatless casserole.

- If you're in a hurry, pre-made deli salads are convenient but a bit pricey for the amount you get. I like to buy a small amount (1/2 to 1 pound) and stretch the quantity, simply by adding a cup of plain boiled pasta or potatoes. Most deli salads like macaroni, potato and cole slaw are swimming in sauce. Now you've got more salad that taste better and has lost its soupy consistency. A win-win situation for sure.

- Have Sunday breakfast any day of the week. I make a triple batch of pancakes or French toast on the weekend, pack three or four in a sandwich baggy and freeze. When you're ready to eat, just pop them in the toaster or microwave for a nice hot breakfast. Cost only pennies compared to the store-bought frozen.

- Don't throw away the juice in canned fruit; add it to Kool-Aid, Jell-O or other fruit juices. Not only does it enhance the flavor and stretch the quantity, you get an extra boost of vitamin C.

- Add an extra can of water to frozen juice concentrate. The flavor is lighter and less acidic. For a spritzer or cooler, add seltzer or ginger ale instead of the extra can of water. Garnish with lemon or lime for a fancier look and extra vitamin C.

- Lemons will produce more juice when squeezed at room temperature rather than cold right out of the refrigerator. If you forget to take them out ahead of time, simply microwave them for a few seconds before squeezing.

- Keep eggs in the carton towards the back of the refrigerator, not in the door. It's the cooler part of the fridge and keeps the eggs fresh longer, especially in the summer and/or when the door is open and closed a lot.

- Use up fresh vegetables like celery, carrots or onions that are on their way down to line your baking pans instead of using a wire rack. They will add lots of flavor to whatever you're cooking and eliminate the need for oil to prevent sticking. Instead of throwing away wilted produce, you'll USE what you otherwise would throw away.

- Lettuce stays crisp and lasts longer when first wrapped (burrito style) in a paper towel. The paper absorbs excess water that causes it to wilt and go brown. Finish by placing in a plastic bag or lettuce bowl.

- Store broccoli in the same manner as lettuce; only poke a few holes in the plastic bag. This allows some airflow through the bag that discourages mildew and decay. Other veggies to store this way: asparagus, string beans, zucchini and peppers.

- Fresh, whole garlic bulbs will last longer when stored in an open container in a cool, dark place. An unbroken bulb will last up to two months. Once you've cracked off a clove, it will last up to ten days. Freeze extra cloves in storage bags and thaw when needed.

- Buy the freshest produce you can. This may mean taking a little more time choosing your fresh fruit and vegetables, but it's well worth the time. Produce should be firm, have bright color and be smooth and dry to the touch. Remember, you're buying it because you want your family to eat it! I was surprised when I spoke to a friend about the produce at a particular store. She said the produce quality was poor and I disagreed. Later I found out she was just grabbing fruit without checking it for bruises or soft spots. Of course, it only took one time for one person at home to bite into a rotten spot and swear off fruit for a year. It's a simple concept, if you want your loved ones to indulge in more healthful choices like fruits and veggies; they've got to taste good!

• Be careful buying bagged fruit. Oranges are the only choice I would even think about buying already bagged. You can't check each piece, and the stores know this. Half the bag is usually badly bruised. I will only buy bagged fruit when the store has slashed the price and I plan to bake with it.

• Use the scale and check the weight of pre-bagged produce like potatoes and onions. Some bags weigh less than others. Take a minute to make sure you're getting as much weight as you're paying for.

• One of my pet peeves is the lonely sandwich bread ends that no one eats. It gets left in the bag to get hard and stale. There has got to be something psychological about not eating the last pieces besides not liking the crust. I found that by placing those pieces at the front of the new bag increases their consumption rate. If that doesn't work, how about using those slices for French toast, stuffing or grilled sandwiches. Season, toast them and cut into squares for croutons. If all else fails, feed the birds!

• Practice rationing. It sounds severe, but it's really a simple concept. Once you've shopped and brought home your groceries, you now have to make sure your family eats it. Fact is, you've got to direct the attention on the foods they should be eating. I've already stated that eating is a physical need with lots of physiological undertones. Do you ever remember times as a kid and fighting over the last piece of chicken or cake? Remember how desirable a particular food became when there wasn't enough to go around? I use that same theory in my house to fool the family. I keep my fresh fruit in the back of the fridge (where no one ever looks), and only put out one piece per family member in the fruit bowl. It quickly gets eaten because it's in full view, and there is a limited supply. Test out this method at home. I'll bet if you fill the bowl with all the fruit, it will all sit until it's soft and mushy. I know you can think of a million times there was just enough food for everyone to get a nice portion for dinner. That night, everyone wanted seconds, right? That's because our minds tells us we want what is unavailable. When folks think there is only a little to go around, it's goes quickly. Get creative and think of how many products you can apply this concept to.

- Invest in a slow cooker. Otherwise known as crock-pots, these devices have been around awhile, and with good reason. They're relatively inexpensive (around $25-$35), last forever, and work wonders on those days you plan on getting home late or just don't want to fuss about dinner. It's like having hired help in the kitchen. Better yet, they don't talk back or complain about the long hours. There's nothing like coming home from work to the wonderful smell of dinner cooking. I still love it when I step through the front door and take a sniff wondering, "hmm, something sure smells good…who cooked?" When I drag myself in the door at the end of the day, I've already forgotten how I quickly threw some frozen meat and veggies in the pot that morning and dashed off. The crock-pot makes inexpensive cuts of meat juicy, tender and flavorful. Use it for stews, soups, beans, roasts—you name it—it can probably be done in a crock-pot. There's no way you can burn your food and you don't have to worry about constant checking and stirring. In the summer they're handy, cause they don't heat up the whole kitchen like the stove does. Sometimes when I'm really short of time, I just throw the meat and some bottled barbecue sauce or a cream soup in the pot—you just can't go wrong! It's worth a little extra money to purchase the crock-pot with the removable ceramic dish that goes straight to the table and is dishwasher safe. More good news about modern-day slow cookers is that you no longer have to pre-brown meat for stews. It's healthy eating because the food cooks in it's own juices, which eliminates the need for heavy seasoning or extra oil. What's not to like…you and a crock-pot…a winning team that can't lose. I dare you to try it and not like it.

- Consider visiting discount warehouse stores, especially for paper products and other non-perishables you can store in bulk. You don't have to join, just go and get a free one-day pass. If you're on a mailing list, you'll most likely receive a free short-term membership card to entice you into the store. Develop a mental list of any items that give you phenomenal savings and only buy those items. Try not to drift.

- Don't always assume no-name or store brands are the cheapest. I have found that some name brands are actually cheaper than the store brand during sale promotions. Prices change from week to week, so you always have to be aware of the price. Comparison-shopping is the only way to make sure. It takes a little longer, but the savings really add up.

- Buying bulk is not always cheaper. I almost bought a ten-pound bag of rice for $4.69, but noticed the five-pound bag was $1.99. 70 cents savings for one item is nothing to snort at. Also, the five-pound bags are lighter, easier to handle and store.

- Speaking of storage, consider whether or not you have the space. Will it get eaten quickly enough, without rotting or attracting bugs? Ask the manager at the supermarket for super-sized, empty jars. Wash and dry thoroughly and store your bulk items there.

- Family packs of meat costs from ten to thirty cents per pound less than smaller sized packages. You don't have to have a large family to save. Once home, separate the meat into meal-sized servings with baggies and freeze.

Frozen Assets

Your freezer can be the key to stretching your groceries to the max. Incorporate some of these easy ways to get the most mileage from the foods you buy. Freezing food is a snap when done correctly. I actually prefer using the cheaper plastic freezer storage bags instead of the zipper-type bags. Vacuum-seal the food you intend to freeze. Airtight packaging maintains the quality and taste of any frozen food and prevents freezer-burn. First, the food goes into sandwich bags so you can take out only how much you need. Then add the wrapped food into freezer bags, shape a funnel at the top and suck out the air. Yes, with your mouth and lungs! Give the bag a spin and twist-tie it closed. I first learned this method when I was a Fresh-Air kid from the Bronx. I went to Pennsylvania for two weeks and stayed with a farming family. This is how they froze their fresh picked produce. I figure if they're farmers, they are the experts and know what they're doing. Believe me, it works like a charm. Who needs expensive vac-seal machines when you already come fully equipped?

- Freeze any leftovers immediately. I don't care if you intend to serve it tomorrow. You can't predict the future, and your schedule may change. How many times have you meant to re-heat those leftovers but didn't? After sitting around in the fridge for a few days, no one wants to eat it. After a week, even the dog turns up his nose at it. So, even if you do serve it the next day, it will still taste fresher than if it sat in the fridge overnight. If you only have enough for one serving, make a frozen dinner with a partitioned microwave safe plastic or paper plates. Slide into a freezer bag and seal.

- If you are cooking extra portions for freezing, remove the meat, pasta or vegetables before they are fully cooked. Seal in freezer bags and cool immediately by immersing the packing in the sink with cold water. If you put hot food in the freezer, the overall temperature will rise and affect the other frozen items there. Leaving the food slightly under-cooked will result in the reheated items being cooked to perfection.

- Meat can be frozen separately on cookie sheets and then transferred to freezer bags. Food won't stick together in the bag and you can take out what you need. I use sandwich bags to individually wrap fresh meat and then transfer the packs to a large freezer bag and vacuum seal.

- Buy quality meat in bulk when it's on sale. You can afford a tender cut like boneless sirloin when it's on sale for under $1.99 per pound. How much did you pay for your last pack of hot dogs? A one-pound package costs about the same, and some brands more! If you don't have the cash or the space to store the whole thing, pool your resources with a friend or relative. Most supermarkets will custom cut your order at no extra charge. At first it may seem like you're spending a lot of money on meat at one time, but once you start to breeze by the meat department during the next few shopping trips, you'll feel great. Sometimes I like to check out the prices of the same meat I bought a week earlier and shake my head sadly at the poor folks that don't know the value of thrift! You're family doesn't have to be the Waltons to benefit by buying food in bulk. Frozen properly, your meat will last and your weekly grocery bill will be considerably lower.

- Let's say the price is $30 for a 15 lb. tender cut of beef like sirloin or eye round. This can be custom cut into a 3-5 lb. roast, 6-8 16 oz. steaks and 5 lbs. ground beef. Individually wrap each steak. The steak can be cubed for stew, sliced for stir-fry or tossed on the grill. In other words, because it's a quality cut it can be fixed almost any way you like. One pound of beef is usually enough for any given meal because there is no bone or waste. The ground beef gets divided into five separate 1 lb. packages or less if you like. Store in sandwich baggies and then into the freezer bag using the farmer 's suck-vac and seal method. This is enough beef for the whole month and beyond for $30. You have at least 5 meals using ground beef, 6-8 meals using the steak and 1 or 2 meals with the roast. So out of 30 days in a month, you could eat beef 15 times. So for an average family of four, this meat should last you two months. Yet, you could easily spend $30 on meat for 2 or 3 dinners if you don't plan. If you wait and buy on impulse, you could pay the usually price of $5 to $7 for the same quality meat (more than triple the sale price!)

- Fall season is harvest time. There will be some great buys at the market now. Buy extra fresh veggies in season (when they taste the best and cost the least) and freeze immediately. This allows you to enjoy the bounty any time of the year. Some foods can be washed and frozen without any further preparation. Others have to be "blanched" before freezing.

Seasonal Fresh Food:

Get the best buys on these items:

Spring: Asparagus, spinach, lettuce, green onion, sweet onion, baby beets, radishes, rhubarb, strawberries, gooseberries, spring greens [dandelion, mustard, watercress, Swiss chard, sprouts, green beans, carrots, leeks, wild mushroom, broccoli, rabe, snow peas, sugar-snap peas, green peas, new potatoes and Brussels sprouts.

Summer: Corn, tomatoes, eggplant, cucumber, zucchini, summer squash, carrots, cantaloupe, musk melons, raspberries, blackberries, blueberries, cherries, peaches, plums, leeks, okra, bell peppers, string beans, Swiss chard, watermelon, nectarines, some varieties of grapes, lima beans, green beans, some varieties of apples, herbs.

Fall: Broccoli, lettuce, spinach, cauliflower, cabbage, garlic, onions, carrots, pumpkin, winter squash [butternut, acorn, turban], hot peppers, apples, pears, Brussels sprouts.

Winter: Parsnips, beets, sweet potatoes, potatoes, citrus fruits, broccoli rabe, cabbage, Belgian endive, escarole, horseradish, Jerusalem artichokes, turnips, celery, celery root, leeks, rutabagas, winter greens [collards, kale, turnip greens, beet greens], winter squash, fennel, onions, garlic, shallots.

- Freezing is usually the preferred method of storing vegetables. However, much of the time and effort of gardening and packing fresh vegetables is wasted simply because people do not take the time to blanch their vegetables before putting them in the freezer. Blanching your vegetables before freezing preserves their color, flavor and nutrition. Blanching stops enzyme action from destroying the fresh flavor of your vegetables. If they are not blanched, vegetables will lose their color and flavor after about four to six weeks of freezer storage. In addition, blanching removes dirt and bacteria. It's very important that blanching be done correctly and that you follow the recommended blanching time for individual vegetables. Under-blanching stimulates the enzyme action that destroys flavor; over-blanching removes color and vitamins. To blanch, bring one gallon of water to a vigorous boil. Drop in only one pound of vegetables at a time so the water can circulate around each piece and kill the enzymes. When the water returns to a boil, start timing. Here are recommended blanching times for the following vegetables:

- Beans (lima)

  2 to 4 minutes

- Beans (snap)

3 minutes

- Corn on cob

  7 to 11 minutes

- Corn

  4 minutes

- Peas (garden or field)

  2 minutes

- Okra

  3 to 4 minutes

- Squash

  3 minutes

You can use the same blanching water for six to 10 batches of the same vegetable. If you are blanching leafy vegetables, use two gallons of boiling water to prevent the leaves from matting together. Once you have blanched your vegetables, remove them from the boiling water. They need to cool as quickly as possible to stop cooking. The best method is to place the vegetables in a pan of ice water. Cool three to four minutes before packing. You are now ready to blanch the next batch. Expect some shrinking of some vegetables when you blanch. This will make them easier to pack. Blanching ensures that fresh vegetables stay fresh in the freezer.

- God is good. Nutritious greens like collards, turnips and spinach don't need to be blanched before freezing. And don't we love them! Simply wash well, cut up and freeze. If you prefer, you can blanch your greens and this will shorten the amount of cooking time. Buy during the summer and fall season when the price is low and freeze for the holidays. You'll be busy enough preparing all the holiday fixin's that can't be done ahead of time. Boil up some turkey wings and drop in the frozen greens. You'll be patting yourself on the back for your foresight. Or you can grow your own collards. Greens are so hardy (just like us); they can withstand any weather conditions and will grow just about anywhere. How do you think this vegetable became such an important staple in our diets way back when? Greens can be grown from spring to fall, all the way to the first frost. Matter of fact, if you let some grown through the first frost, they will be more tender and taste sweeter.

- Avoid buying frozen food with ice crystals on the package. This is a sign that they've been thawed and re-frozen, which mean the food could no longer be fresh. The nutrient content has certainly been compromised and the taste will be inferior.

- Keep extra loaves of bread in the freezer. Bread and baked goods in general get a stale flavor when stored in the refrigerator. In the warm summer months, bread gets moldy fast when left on a warm kitchen counter or breadbox. With the price of bread rising steadily, buy extra when it's on sale and freeze. Take out of the freezer ½ hour before you are ready to use. Bread thaws pretty quickly. If you're in a hurry, you can pop slices into the toaster for a few seconds to speed up the process. Once thawed, eat within a couple days.

- Some foods just don't freeze well. Fried foods tend to taste warmed over when reheated. Cucumbers and salad greens turn limp and soggy when thawed.

- Label and date your packages before you put them in the freezer. Don't rely on your memory, especially if you make good use of your freezer and keep it well stocked. Use a permanent marker and labels or masking tape.

- Another idea for labeling your frozen food is to color code by season. Use green labels for spring, yellow for summer, orange for fall and blue for winter. When the season changes, you'll know to finish up all the previous season's frozen items.

Expose the Pros

Ever notice how quickly manufacturers jump on certain marketing trends? Well, you can bet your bottom dollar those are the trends that give them the most bang for their marketing buck. That means we as consumers pay the price for their hefty returns. It's the job of manufacturers and advertisers to make a profit by any means necessary. They have spent millions investigating what, when, how and why people buy what they buy. They're the experts, but you can win this battle just by being an educated consumer.

- Don't pay the price for "light" drinks or juice "cocktails". I can't count how many products now have a "light" line. That doesn't have to be a bad thing in these days of a more health conscious society. Unfortunately, light can mean anything from lighter in color to lower in calories. Most "light" drinks are expensive; contain more water and less juice. That's right, you're paying more for less. That's a definite violation of the thrifty rule. Notice how the first words on the label are Peach or Mango or Grapefruit, but they contain as little as 5% juice. You can really get ripped off if you don't read the labels. If you prefer the lighter flavor of "light" drinks, make your own! Simply add water or seltzer to the original product. You can do this by the glass or container. You'll get more and pay less. That's the thrifty ticket.

- Manufacturers pay for shelf space on the supermarket aisles. Products placed on the shelf that is eye-level to the average person costs them the most, and they are quite happy to pass their fees on to you. They understand human nature and that people tend to first grab what is right in front of them. Look high and low on the shelves for the products that cost less.

- Department stores pay close attention to what aisle products reside, and your supermarket is no different. Notice how the staples like milk, eggs or bread are located far away from the entrance. When you drop by to pickup just a few items, you'll have to pass many aisles and resist the tempting displays on the way there. If you can't keep your eyes on the prize, don't bring your purse. Put just enough money for what you intend to purchase in your pocket to eliminate any impulse purchases.

- Just because a product is displayed at the aisle ends doesn't mean it's on sale. True, this area is where they sometimes store extra sale merchandise, but it's also a prime spot to stock overflow. Many people just assume all the products placed here are on sale. As you are waiting on the checkout line, these large displays entice us to grab one (more thing you didn't need).

- Pay close attention to quantity. The price may be the same, but the package size has been reduced. It started first with canned goods and candy bars, but others are joining the bandwagon. The average can size used to be 16 ounces, now reduced to 14 or 15 ounces. They think they're slick because the size reduction is too slight to be noticed at first glance. Number one thrifty rule, always read labels.

- Breakfast cereals are heavily advertised toward children. Advertisements cost them a lot of money, so those cereals cost more. Kids will beg for their favorites and you'll pay out the nose. Unfortunately, it's often the box they are more interested in or the cheap toy inside rather than the cereal taste. Try the bagged cereal clones or the store brands. If your kids really put up a fuss, buy the cereal once and save the box. Refill with the clones. Most likely, no one will notice. Another option is to buy a large refillable container and store your cereals there. No box, no proof.

- Convenience packaging may save time, but costs up to three times as much as bulk. Don't bother with individually wrapped snacks when you can wrap your own at home using plastic sandwich baggies. Cut up your own veggies and shred your own cheese, unless it's for a special occasion and you just don't have the time. Make jello or pudding in disposable plastic cups for grab and go snacking.

- Shop alone. Bringing the kids will often make you buy products you otherwise wouldn't. They sneak things into the cart, too! Brightly colored boxes dazzle kids and adults alike. Distractions can make you forget items. Certain colors make you feel warm and fuzzy, and all of a sudden you gotta have it. Advertisers have spent a lot of money investigating what makes people buy. When you're alone, it's easier to concentrate on your plan.

- Check expiration dates. I learned this lesson the hard way. The supermarkets in my neighborhood were shameful. Without checking the merchandise, I bought some eggs, bacon, milk and deli meat. The very next day the food was spoiled. I checked the expiration dates, and they were dated a week earlier. The bacon was dated a month back! If you have a supermarket like that near you, do what I did…call the Health Department and boycott that store. You know how it is, the poorer the neighborhood, the lower the quality the food. However, the food sold there is not discounted, it's the same price as the quality food sold in the upscale neighborhoods. Store managers are betting that the locals don't have transportation to get to the better markets across town, so they just rip us off. The meat is on the verge of spoiling, the produce substandard, and bugs in the flour. Why do we still shop there? This scenario is being repeated all over America, but the real shame is that WE TAKE IT. We will go back to that store that has ripped us off or treated us like second-class citizens and continue to spend our hard-earned money there. DON'T DO IT. These places can only exist if we support them. When will we rally together and turn our attention to the real enemies in our camps? (Whew, all that from expiration dates?)

Seasonal Savings

Retail stores have a set cycle of price reductions on various products at different times of the year. Use this guide below to learn when to look for the best deals on a variety of merchandise.

December 26 through February:

- Area rugs
- Blankets, quilts
- Candles, books, briefcases
- Children's clothes
- China, glassware
- Christmas decorations, wrapping paper and artificial trees
- Furs
- Hats, gloves, coats, boots
- Home furnishings
- Jewelry
- Linens, curtains
- Minor appliances
- Toys

March through May

- Baby Clothing
- Garden supplies
- Housewares
- Lingerie
- Luggage
- Mattresses
- Painting supplies
- Shoes
- Space heaters
- Sweaters, Winter Wear

June through August

- Appliances
- Back to school specials
- Bicycles
- Building supplies
- Carpeting
- Cosmetics
- Curtains, drapes
- Fabrics, craft materials
- Floor coverings

- Men's clothing
- Sports equipment
- Summer Wear
- Tires, auto accessories

September through December

- Air conditioners
- Automobiles (outgoing models)
- Bicycles
- Cookware, dishes
- Fall fashions
- Fishing equipment
- Furniture
- Garden equipment
- Major Appliances
- Outdoor furniture and grills
- Storewide clearances
- Vacation plans
- Happy shopping!

Chapter 4: Natural Beauty

The so-called "beauty experts" are spouting what our ancestors have always known, pure and simple is the best way to go. Nature provides us with a bountiful harvest of ingredients to keep you looking young and fresh. Lately, there has been an explosion of holistic health companies and products. Everywhere you look there is natural this and herbal that. People are going hog-wild over the same stuff my grandmother use to cook up. It's become a huge, lucrative market. No wonder, the prices of these products are astronomical.

Some people feel that having lots of products in the bathroom mean they take good care of themselves. (Regardless of the fact that half of the stuff is never used.) Reducing the amount of products you buy will save you money and time on your daily maintenance routine, and produce beautiful results. Buying ready-made creams can cost a small fortune. Why buy them when you can create your own, personalized formulas.

I've been mixing up my own beauty concoctions for years. Someone once called me a "concoctress" and I thought the name was fitting. I'll show you how to become one too, and you'll see how easy it is to stir up your own blends and brews. It isn't costly, because many of the ingredients you'll need can be found right in your kitchen, garden or bathroom.

Take some time out to try these super beauty routines and body balms. Get together with your best buddy and indulge in a "spa-at-home" night. Pampering yourself will uplift your spirit, boost your ego and it's fun. It can be a time of self-affirmation, relaxation and physical renewal. Get in touch with your senses. Girlfriend, it you don't do it for yourself, who will?

Important Guidelines for the "Concoctress"

1. Before using any potion, apply a small amount of your concoction to the inside of the elbow or wrist to test skin sensitivity.

2. Avoid applying any mixtures near the eye area or around mucus membranes.

3. Use plastic caps on hair concoctions to build up body heat and increase penetration into the hair shaft. This will also keep mixtures from running onto face. Add a terry cloth headband if necessary to further protect eyes. Make your own by cutting a sash in half from an old terrycloth robe.

4. Save plastic and/or glass jars and tops to mix and house your brews. Many of them will keep for weeks in the refrigerator. Do not use aluminum receptacles for mixing, boiling or storage, as certain ingredients can cause a chemical reaction with the metal. If you must use metal, enamel or steel pots are preferred.

5. Herbs and flower leaves can be found at your local florist and health food stores. Better still, grow your own kitchen herb garden. All you need is a sunny window. Pick up small inexpensive herb plants or seeds and follow directions on care label or seed packets. Most beneficial varieties include parsley, rosemary, chamomile, thyme, sage, lavender and mint. These herbs can be used fresh or dried. They can be concentrated by mixing with alcohol, vinegar or water, and can be made into ointments for application to the skin. For external use on the skin or scalp, they are prepared by mixing the powdered herb with lard or lanolin. With the exception of lavender and chamomile, the dried, crushed herbs above can be bought from the 99 cents spice line.

Herb Care: To dry fresh herbs, clip a small bunch with sharp scissors. Tie with string, rubber band or twist tie and hand upside down from a hanger in a cool place away from direct sunlight. Or you can freeze fresh herbs with the suc-vac method. It is debatable whether herbs need to be blanched before freezing. Blanching is recommended if you intend to keep herbs in the freezer for six months or longer. The procedure is simple. Simply grip several stalks of the herb with tongs and quickly swish them in a skillet of boiling water. Spread the herbs on a towel to air cool. When cool and dry, the herbs can be frozen. They will lose some color, but not their restorative qualities.

Aromatic Waters: Use pure (distilled, rain or spring) water blended with fragrant herbs. These make wonderful skin toners, hair rinses or body wash. Simply add 1 cup of dried herbs to a pint of pure water in a quart size jar with a tight fitting lid. Keep the jar in a convenient place away from sunlight. Shake once or twice daily for two weeks. Strain the mixture through a stocking into small jars with tight fitting lids. Suggested herbs for aromatic waters are rose petals, rosemary, aloe, chamomile, lavender and citrus fruits.

Decoction: Decoction is the extraction of mineral and principles of plants by boiling in water. After boiling for a half hour, they are allowed to stand for another half hour. The resulting liquid is filtered into jars. These can be mixed with olive or mineral oil, dollar lotions or plain vegetable lard for application onto the body.

Skin Care

We people of color have been blessed with skin that is thicker, more elastic, smoother and less prone to wrinkles than our Caucasian counterparts. Sill, good looks really do come about the old fashioned way, from the inside out. A beautiful person is one who is sure of themselves, healthy and toned. Don't let the media tell you any different. How you feel about yourself shows on you.

- Want silky smooth skin? Try using a loofah during your bath or shower. The loofah (sometimes called a cucumber strainer) is a natural sponge that is actually the seedpod of a plant called a gorge. The loofah will slouch off dead skin and improve blood circulation to the skin. They come in various sizes, even a bath mitt, and are available in most drug, discount and department stores. The cheapest ones I've found (around a buck or two) are in discount stores like Wal-Mart. Drug stores were the most expensive, charging up to five dollars for the same item!

- The cheapest way to achieve great skin is to drink lots of water. Water cleanses your body of toxins and excess oils that can develop into pimples. Water moisturizes from the inside and will keep your skin dewy and soft. If you live in an area where your tap water is sub standard, it will be well worth the money to invest in a water pitcher with a built-in filter. Boiling the water first will also help remove pollutants. Some locations with admittedly bad water have provided vending machines outside of supermarkets that dispense filtered water. Bring your own plastic containers and fill for a fraction of the cost of store-bought water.

- God bless our ash. You heard me. People of color don't show their age, and I believe our skin wears so well because we've been lotioning up from the day we were born. I know you've tried to go without it sometimes, but that ash tells on you, don't it? We rarely miss a day without it. You can buy cheap aloe or cocoa butter based lotion for 99 cents a bottle and bump up its effectiveness. Add ½ cup of mineral or olive oil and the contents of three to five vitamin E soft capsules.

- Fine ground cornmeal makes a great facial scrub with combined with your favorite beauty soap (oily skin) or oil (dry skin). If you can't find the fine-ground cornmeal, stone-ground, regular cornmeal will do. Just be careful and massage GENTLY, as the regular cornmeal can be more abrasive. You don't want to your skin to be raw.

- Witch Hazel works wonders as a skin toner and astringent. Oily skin will benefit from its cleansing, toning features year round. Dry skin will find it refreshing in the warm weather, and will keep the skin free of blemishes caused by dirt and sweat.

- Steam your face with fragrant waters for a refreshing, quick facial. Fill a bowl with steaming water and add 1) calming herbs such as lavender or chamomile 2) herbs to pick you up like peppermint or rosemary or citrus fruit or 3) soothing herb like eucalyptus or rose petals. Cover your head with a towel and hold your face directly over the steamy bowl. After five minutes, splash your face with cold water and pat dry.

- To reduce the size of a zit quickly, apply tomato paste directly on the pimple. Rinse off after 15 minutes.

- Blemish buster. Make a paste of ½ teaspoon of dried thyme, 1-teaspoon cider vinegar and 1 teaspoon of lemon juice. Apply on pimples for ½ hour. Rinse thoroughly.

- Makeup can enhance your natural beauty or make you look like a clown. You can spend a fortune on expensive skin-care systems and makeup. Unlike clothes, once you've tried them, they are un-returnable. The result is a collection of all sorts of makeup and beauty products, of which your probably only use a few. This happens when we're not sure what to buy or what looks good on us. For women of color, it is very hard to get a good match to your complexion without trying it on first. Many of the drug store varieties tend to make our skin ashy or ruddy, though that trend is slowly changing. If you decide to buy there, inquire about their refund policy on makeup. Some stores are making a change in that area. Or, you can eliminate this problem by going to department stores with makeup counters and consultants, and get a free makeover to boot! Though the salesperson may try to sell you a ton of products, you don't have to buy them. You can try out different types of foundations (liquid, cream or powders) and colors. Find out what colors complement your skin tone and settle on a basic plan. Go in with a clean face and speak to the consultant about your skin type and what products will do best on it. It's their job to serve you, whether you buy anything or not, so don't let yourself be intimidated. The only product I would recommend making an investment in (meaning you'll pay more than at the drug store) is with your foundation and powder. It's the canvas on which you will paint, and should be flawless.

- Remove all traces of your makeup before retiring to bed at night. Every day, we subject our faces to air pollutants, dirt, sweat and oil, in addition to your make up. Going to bed with a clean face gives your skin a break and allows it to breath. Petroleum jelly, mineral oil, even vegetable oil works fine as well as old-fashioned cold cream. Work the substance all over face, neck and around eye area. After wiping off your makeup with soft tissue, wash with a beauty soap, rinse away all traces of the soap and moisturize. Your skin will reflect your care.

Facial Treatments

There are many recipes for facials that come right out of your kitchen or bathroom. The expensive health spas use these same natural ingredients. Try one out and see an immediate difference in your mirror. What's even better is that you can use these masks anywhere on your body where skin breakouts or blemishes are a problem.

DRY SKIN

- Honey & Oatmeal. Mix 1-tablespoon quick oatmeal (not instant) to 1/8 cup honey and stir into a paste. Apply over your clean face and leave on for 10 minutes. Rinse with warm water and follow with moisturizer.

- Oatmeal & Milk. Soothe and cleanse your skin with this mixture. Mix 1-tablespoon quick oatmeal with enough milk (about 1/8 cup) to make a thick paste. Apply over clean face and leave on for 10 minutes. Rinse with warm water.

- Cocoa Butter & Vitamin E. This is my favorite for dry skin, especially in the winter months. Break open a few vitamin E soft capsules and apply under eyes and on lips. Massage 100% cocoa butter (comes in stick and cream form) and massage into clean skin, all the way back into the hairline and neck. Lleave on for 10 minutes and rinse with plain warm water.

- Oatmeal & Water. This facial treatment will tighten skin and reduce fine lines. Mix 1-tablespoon quick oatmeal with enough water to make a thick paste. Be prepared for it to really tighten on your face as it dries. Wash off thoroughly with warm water. Follow with moisturizer.

- Olive Oil & Milk. Mix 1 ounce powdered milk with 1 ounce of olive oil to make a paste. Apply to face, avoiding eye area and leave on for 10 to 15 minutes. Rinse with lukewarm water.

OILY SKIN

- Cleanse face thoroughly. Whip an egg white till it thickens and peaks. Apply to face, avoiding eyes. Leave on for 10 minutes, rinse with warm water.

- Plain yogurt is a good treatment for oily skin. Simply apply onto clean face, and leave on for 5 minutes. Rinse with plain water.

- Mash a small tomato into a pulpy paste and apply to face, avoiding eye area. Leave on for 10 minutes and rinse with lukewarm water.

The Bath

The bath has long been recognized as a holistic remedy for everything from relieving stress to itchy skin. Cleopatra was known to soak in tubs filled with milk. You can prepare your own herbal bath in the privacy of your own bathroom. These baths can stimulate or calm the mind, open pores, rejuvenate the skin or relieve pain. Try some of these ancestral recipes and indulge yourself like royalty.

THE BASIC RULES

1. Make your bath water warm, not hot. Very hot water will dry out and damage your skin. Lukewarm, even cool water is best.

2. Old stockings or pantyhose make perfect receptacles for your herbal mixtures. You can use more than just the toe, as long as the runs in the stockings aren't so wide that the filling will come out. Cut an eight-inch length of stocking and knot at one end, fill and tie a knot at the other. Leave enough length at one end to open a hole to fit over the tub faucet. The stocking will be hung on the faucet in such a way that the water will run through it as you fill the tub.

BEAUTY MIX: Mix ½ cup thyme, ½ cup rosemary, ½ cup dried mind and ½ cup lavender flowers.
REFRESHING MIX: 1-cup eucalyptus branches or leaves with ¼ cup mint leaves.
MUSCLE RELIEVER: Add equal parts sage and strawberry leaves. Add ¼ cup Epson salts to the bath water.
ITCHY SKIN: Add 1-cup vinegar to your bath water.

SATIN DOLL BODY TREATMENT

Check this out one night when you have nothing else planned (or better still, when you DO have something planned)! Works miracles on dry, ashy, rough skin. You won't believe your skin after this treatment, it will feel brand new.

1. Put 1-cup baking soda or sugar in a bowl.

2. Add enough water to make a paste.

3. Set aside a small bowl ¼ cup cornmeal.

4. Standing in a dry tub, rub sugar or baking soda mixture onto your body and massage with your hands. Start from your feet and work your way up to your chin using circular motions.

5. Rub cornmeal onto feet, elbows and knees and massage in gently.

6. Rinse off with lukewarm water.

7. Wash thoroughly using a beauty soap (like Tone, Dove or Caress),

8. After shower, while still wet, rub body liberally with heavy lotion or oil.

9. Wrap up in a robe or towel. Once your body is dry, apply a second coat of your favorite lotion or perfumed oil.

10. Add heavy moisture to (petroleum jelly, cocoa butter) onto knees, elbows and feet. Put on cotton socks for at least one hour or better still, overnight.

Watch Your Mouth

What good is a great face without a winning smile? Taking care of your teeth can save you a fortune in dentist bills, not to mention long, painful hours in the chair. Follow these tips for pretty pucker power.

Brush your teeth for 5 minutes. It's the recommended time (according to the Dental Association) to get your teeth really clean, but most of us don't brush that long. If you actually set a timer, you'll see how long a five-minute brushing really is. Make sure to brush the inside of the teeth, as well as the outside and gums.

- Brush your tongue. I didn't grow up with this habit, but now I never go a day without it. You'll be shocked at how much gunk comes off your tongue every day. This practice makes for a pretty pink tongue instead of a coated white one (which should only look that way if your sick!). My dentist has told me that tongue scrubbing reduces plaque and tartar buildup. I guarantee once your try this, you won't be satisfied with just brushing your teeth anymore. Your mouth will feel 100% cleaner and your breath will stay fresh much longer. Simply brush your tongue with your toothbrush first in one direction and rinse, repeat in the other direction. Rinse your toothbrush thoroughly after each use with hot water, or dab your brush in a small cup of peroxide.

- Baking Soda makes a good toothpaste. Simply dip your wet toothbrush into a spoonful.

- Make your own whitening toothpaste by adding a dash of lemon juice or hydrogen peroxide to 1 teaspoon of baking soda.

- Lip balm or chap stick should be a staple in your pocketbook. The perfect size for any purse, it's not just for relieving dry, cracked lips.

Since it's main ingredient is paraffin wax, it can be used in other ways. Swipe it across your bare eyebrows, and using an old toothbrush, tame, shape and shine them. Use them in a pinch like hair wax or gel. The wax holds down those wispy baby fines around your hairline and gives you a finished, polished look.

CHAPPED LIPS TREATMENT

This is best done before bedtime. Wake up to soft, sexy lips.

1. Coat lips with petroleum jelly or lip balm. Leave on for 5 minutes

2. Using an old toothbrush, brush lips gently.

3. Wipe off flaky, dry skin with a warm, damp washcloth.

4. Crack open a soft capsule of vitamin E and smooth onto lips. Do not rub off.

Hands, Feet & Nails

Our hands are exposed to more sun, chemicals and harsh elements than any other part of our body. We express ourselves with our hands, and adorn them with precious metals and expensive jewels. Yet, we tend to neglect the care of this very important extremity. Our hands easily get dry, ashy and look older than the rest of our body. We cover our nails with everything and anything, but what about the real nail underneath? Do they look good enough to go bare, or do you feel forced to cover them up? Our feet, though not exposed as much as the hands, will benefit from the same treatments we use on our hands. So when it's time to uncover them (at home or in public) they'll be in top condition.

- Buy a pumice stone. Cost only about a buck and is available at most drug and department stores. It's a lava rock that is great for maintaining soft feet, reducing corns and calluses, rough knees and elbows. Gently rub over those areas every time your bathe and moisturize afterwards. The key word here is "gently". You don't have to scrub hard, the pumice will do the work. I told my friend about this, and she reported later that her skin was rubbed raw. Turned out she was using it on the thin skin around her ankles and was scrubbing hard. Once she corrected her method, she was very happy with the results. Please, only use the pumice on rough skin and you'll see a difference in a matter of days! This works so well and is so easy, even my husband got on the program. It works a lot better and is much safer than trimming off that dead skin with a razor, thank you very much!

- Make a paste with baking soda and water. Scrub your hands and nails with the mixture. This will brighten yellow nails and soften skin. Rinse and follow with a generous amount of lotion or oil.

- Use an emery board instead of a metal file. It's much gentler on the nails. Always file your nails in one direction towards the center on either side. Don't saw back and forth, it will split the nail.

- To condition nails, soak them in warm olive oil for 10 or 15 minutes. Rinse with warm water.

- Remove old nail polish stains. Take ½ of a lemon and twist on the fingertips of the opposite hand as if they were a juicer. Switch to the other hand, rinse and moisturize.

- For a quick, natural manicure, file nails, then dampen a nail whitening pen and run under nail tips.

- Refresh and revive hot, tired feet quickly with a spritz of Witch Hazel. When dry, lightly dust with talcum powder or cornstarch.

- Are your dogs barking? Try this tingling foot soak. Add mint leaves to a pan of cold water and soak your feet for 10 to 20 minutes.

- Hot Rock Foot Massage: Find a smooth, round stone that fits comfortably in the palm of your hand. Apply a thin coat of olive or vegetable oil to the stone. Heat the rock up for 10 minutes in the oven. The rock should not be too hot to the touch, but use an oven mitt when removing from the oven anyway. Now you can either rub the warm stone over the bottom of your foot or simply place the rock on the ground and roll your foot over it. Heaven!

- Cucumber is a natural astringent and can rejuvenate your feet. In summer, when cucumbers are abundant and cheap, soak your feet in a pan with cool water laced with thin slices of 1 or 2 cucumbers.

THE COMPLETE HAND OR FOOT TREATMENT

Before bedtime, soak feet and/or hands in soapy water. Scrub calluses and rough spots thoroughly but gently with a pumice stone. Make your cornmeal scrub and massage all over hands and/or feet. Apply petroleum jell or heavy oil or lotion and cover with cotton socks or gloves. Wake up to soft, smooth hands and feet. Clip or file nails (toenails straight across), polish and go.

Our Hair

What can I say about OUR hair? I know this, most of us have a love—hate relationship with it. We know we should be proud of our natural hair, but get confused by the images portrayed by the media. We sabotage ourselves with terms like "good" hair. We want our men to keep their eyes off Caucasian women, then try to emulate them. We compare ourselves with the European idea of beauty, i.e., skin and hair color, hair straightness, etc.

I recently wore my hair natural for a few years and still experienced discrimination. It's been a long time since I wore the popular afro in the 60's, but people's reactions haven't changed much. I still found some sisters looking at me like I should be ashamed to be in the street with my hair that way. My own mother still doesn't understand how I think my hair is attractive that way. I am happy to report that my hair was healthier than it ever was and grew much faster. I had endless options for hairstyles. I could go from bone straight to 'fro and every texture in between, whenever I felt like it. Loving my hair in its natural state was a strong, self-accepting experience. I still fluxgate from light perms to natural (cause I love to change my hair), but it's strictly my choice, not someone's idea of how I "should" look. I now know my "naps" are beautiful, versatile, and all mine!

How you wear your hair is strictly your business. Celebrate that fact that our hair comes in a variety of textures, tones, thickness and lengths. Regardless of your style preference, there are a few basic principles that apply to us all.

- Choose hair tools that are appropriate for your hair type. The thicker your hair, the wider the teeth of your comb should be. This will minimize hair breakage. Thank God these combs are now available. Remember the old "afro combs"? I know now why we used to have to "blow out" our hair in order to use them back in the 60's. Those combs were much too fine to get through our Afro's. We suffered with them until the "afro pick" emerged and gave us some relief. Today, you can find a wide variety of combs and picks. Kids will really appreciate your efforts also. I remember all too well the dread of getting my hair done and the feeling that something was wrong with my hair cause my mom couldn't get a comb through it. Now I know we just didn't have the proper tools.

- Don't waste your money on "hair food" products that promise to grow hair. These products don't "feed" hair; they just add greasy weight, making it difficult to hold a style. Normal hair growth is approximately ¼ " to ½ " per month. A healthy diet is the only food you need for healthy hair.

- Brushes should have natural bristles and be used on dry hair only. Our hair is very fragile, especially when wet. Some beauticians claim you don't ever have to brush your hair to keep it healthy, only comb it. It's all a matter of preference, but important information if you've experienced problems with breakage and you've been brushing your hair wet.

- Keep your hair clean. Please don't believe that old saying that dirt makes your hair grow. We're not talking vegetation here. If it smells, won't hold a set, is catching lint or looks matted, the only remedy is to wash it! That's right, honey, it ain't working if it's dirty.

- Use shampoos that are designed for your hair type. Generally, shampoos made for White folks are designed to strip the oil from the scalp and hair. Our hair needs the opposite effect. One that keeps the scalp lubricated and the hair soft. Look for shampoos that moisturize and contain natural ingredients.

- Condition your hair after washing. Conditioners help your hair hold in moisture and allow combing out with minimal breakage. Look for ones with hydrolyzed animal or vegetable protein…or better still, make your own using the formulas on the following pages.

- Have your hair trimmed regularly. Every three months is the average recommendation from the experts, especially if your hair is chemically altered or colored. You don't have to drastically cut it, but your ends need trimming to avoid breakage up the hair shaft. That means if you don't trim it, it will break off anyway. So if you're trying to grow your hair, you've got to cut it. Those dry, brittle ends won't hold a curl and look frizzy.

- Don't grease your scalp. Stop yelling, I know our hair does need some oil and moisture. But heavy gels and pomades globbed directly onto your scalp clog the pores, slows down hair growth and attracts dirt and lint. Instead, use light, natural oils that allow your scalp to breathe. Brush or comb hair from the roots all the way to the ends to distribute the oil evenly throughout your hair.

- Wear a satin sleep cap or silk scarf to bed. It will reduce hair breakage at night, and helps hold your style longer. If you're a restless sleeper you're probably scrubbing your head around on your pillow. Or try covering your pillow with a satin pillowcase.

- Decrease the use of electric hair appliances, especially if your hair is relaxed. Daily use of a curling iron can mean the difference between long, healthy hair and short, damaged hair. If you find that you must use the iron daily, you should consult your hairdresser about a new cut or style that will last you more than one day! Also, make sure your iron is temperature controlled. Set the temperature as low as possible, while still getting your do done.

- A healthier alternative to the curling iron is wet setting relaxed hair. Your set and style will last longer and your hair will be soft and shiny. Hood dryers are available at moderate cost in discount and department stores ($25-$30, the price of one visit to the salon) and last a long time.

- Dump the sponge rollers on relaxed hair. Not only do they break your hair off (unless you faithfully use end papers), the curls come out tight and unruly. Use smooth plastic rollers with large bobby pins to get a sleek, professional looking style.

- Natural hair wearers: want straight hair occasionally but don't want to perm it? Don't bother putting that comb on the stove. High heat from a blow dryer (use a comb attachment) and curling with an electric iron will do the job and still leave you with some body. If you want to wear your hair straight all the time, perming will be a healthier alternative than daily straightening and hot curling.

- Don't perm children's hair. Kiddie perms still contain strong chemicals. If they are not done correctly, they can damage the hair beyond repair. It's not worth the risk. I remember the embarrassment I felt when my brothers and their friends would pass the kitchen as I was getting my hair fried. Oh my, especially when they spied you with half your head straight and the other half nappy. I grew up ashamed of my natural hair, and wouldn't dare step out into the street "kinky". We're still passing that message along when we insist on perming our girls' hair. There are so many lovely styles that young kids (and adults) can wear with their hair natural. Get that blow dryer with the comb attachment to make it more manageable. This will promote healthy, fast growing hair she'll be proud of. It will instill a strong self-image of her. Let her know that her natural hair is beautiful, along with all the rest of her!

Hair Remedies

Dry Hair Treatment:

Work 1 tablespoon of plain yogurt into your hair after shampooing. Allow to sit for 1 minute. Rinse thoroughly.

Dandruff Treatment:

Soak a cotton ball in antiseptic mouthwash (like Listerine). Make small sections in your unwashed hair and rub the cotton ball down the part. Replace the cotton ball as needed. Do this over your entire head then massage gently with your fingertips. Let sit for 10 minutes. Shampoo and rinse hair well. Repeat this treatment every two weeks for a month or two, and your dandruff should disappear.

Itchy Scalp:

Boil 2 tablespoons of dried parsley 1-cup fresh parsley in 1 quart of water for 15 minutes. When cool, strain through a stocking or cheesecloth into a glass jar. Use this mixture as a final rinse after shampooing.

Purifying Lemon Rinse:

Even though you wash your hair regularly, styling products, shampoos and conditioners leave a residue, eventually resulting in dull hair that's hard to manage. Every other month, use this rinse to completely remove any buildup that clog the scalp and slow normal growth. Mix 2 ounces of lemon juice to 1 cup of water. After shampooing, pour or spray this mixture over hair and let dry naturally. Follow with a hot oil treatment (see below) for healthy sheen and maximum control.

Deep Hair Cleaner:

Add 2 tablespoons of baking soda to ¼ cup of your favorite shampoo and wash as usual.

Instant Conditioner:

Work 2 tablespoons of mayonnaise into hair and scalp and let sit for 1 minute. Massage in for 30 seconds. This will add moisture and protein to the hair and make it very soft.

Color Enhancer:

Sage rinse will keep your hair color vibrant and soften gray hair. Boil 1 ounce into 1 quart of water for 15 minutes and strain into jar after cool. Use as a final rinse after rinsing out the shampoo. Do not wash out.

Hot Oil Conditioner:

Massage warm olive oil into hair and scalp. Cover your head with a plastic cap and sit under a dryer or out in the sun for 15 minutes. An alternative is to wrap hair in hot towel over head for 30 minutes (you'll have to reheat the towel a few times—in the microwave or with hot water).

Oily Scalp & Hair Treatment:

Mix 4 teaspoons of lemon juice or vinegar in 5 ounces of water. Use as a final rinse after shampooing. Do not rinse out.

Natural Setting Lotion:

Boil 2 tablespoons of rosemary in 1 quart of water for 15 minutes. Allow to cool and strain into plastic spray bottle. Spritz clean, damp hair and set. This mixture adds body and luster to the hair, with an added bonus of dandruff control.

Chapter 5: Family Matters

The current shift of focus on the family in America is long overdue. Parents are finding the many hours it takes to make ends meet financially have taken a heavy toll on the quality of their family life. Fortunately, it is possible to enhance your family life and increase the household earning power, all in the same fell swoop. Let's face it, most of us haven't got enough time or money to waste. Living on a budget has become a necessity and sticking to it can seem impossible, with growing kids, appetites and prices!

Raising our kids to be well-rounded, happy, productive members of society is just about the thriftiest move any parent can make. If you shirk your responsibilities when the kids are young, you are sure to pay double later. For some of our youth, later comes too late to save them. Think of the pain and suffering of parents of troubled kids. Think of the negative time you'll spend down the road and financial burden you may bear if your kid is in trouble with the law. We've got to be able to achieve our goals and raise our kids in a world with different dangers, less community help and expensive diversions. However, there are resources out there that can be tapped, you just got to know where to look.

Obstacles can be the challenges we can get around, go under or through. We can model this concept to our kids by sharing our own trials with them and how to deal with them. Demonstrate through positive action how each obstacle can be the means of strengthening their character and determination. Parents are the most influential role models in their children's lives. We can help them empower themselves in a way that honors their spirit.

Within our family units exist an infinite value that is priceless. It stands before us in the form of our children. Let's help our kids to understand what things are really important to us. Our actions, not our words, are what they will remember. Including your kids in the daily process of running a household will help them develop skills and make you a team. This teamwork can increase your family's potential for additional earnings, and decreases the need to spend elsewhere.

Outside of our homes there is more groundwork to be done. It is only at the grass roots level that long-lasting change will come. It is an absolute travesty the way we treat our brothers and sisters. The media loves portraying us in the way some of us insist on behaving. Our girls mimic the sexual promiscuity on video networks, and our boys think it's cool to be a roughneck. They call each other dogs, bitches, ho's and thugs. Young mother's in the street, calling their children stupid asses and cursing at them like sailors. Slapping and shutting down their kids before they've even reached school age. It's necessary for us to realize that we as a people must come together on our own. The White man has neither intention nor interest in lifting us up. We've got to begin healing and loving each other and ourselves before we as a people can ever become prosperous.

Back in the day, our people recognized the need for community. Today, we are under the illusion that being self-sufficient is a desirable trait. Our neighborhoods are suffering under that illusion. We've bought into the outward show of prosperity on a personal level, with clothes, cars and other short-lived, material purchases. Let us not forget the priceless value of nurturing our communities, as well as our families.

For parents, the quickest way to feel better about the struggle is to know you are not alone. Get together with other parents, share information and resources. This will increase your success with your kids. They'll be surrounded by those who care and aren't afraid to express it. Let's take a look back at our lives, our roots and most of all, our children. If we truly believe they are our future, what investments are we making in them now? What messages are we sending to them? Parents can get so busy making ends meet, they forget the value of time spent with our youth (your own or somebody else's). And if you're not already doing it, family dinners, neighborhood outings and games are inexpensive ways to spend time with them. Add plain old communication along with discipline and loving guidance and you've got a winning formula to building up the up and coming. Being too busy to properly train and raise our kids brings long-term, disastrous results. Let's not wait until we are forced to take notice of them, whether it is as the victim or initiator of a crime or some other tragedy.

Sometimes that means turning toward your neighbor and sharing, other times that means going it alone. Believe me, once others start seeing you reaping the rewards, they'll want to know how you're doing it. When they ask, don't hold back, spill all the beans!

- Allow your kids in the kitchen. With supervision, kids can make Jell-O, cookies or help make a meal. It's time spent together and a chore gets done at the same time. I know you can get things done quicker without them at first. Make the investment now in the early years and I guarantee you'll be glad down the road, when you really do need their help in the kitchen.

- Rotate your kids' toys. This is a great idea to incorporate when they take in the mother load, like Christmas and birthdays. You know how they get a bunch of toys, but are only interested in two or three at first. (The ones they're not so interested in wind up getting tore up or pieces get lost.) Put the ones they've don't show much interest in away from sight. When they start getting bored with the ones they are using, bring out the stored ones and put the others away. This will keep toys in better condition longer and keep them from whining for something new.

- Start a toy exchange with a friend or neighbor with children of the same age.

- Make your own play kitchen. Make a stove, sink and cabinets out of large, old boxes. Color with crayons or paint with non-toxic paint. Save empty food containers to stock the cabinets.

- Store old or stained dresses, shoes and junk jewelry and keep in a "dress up" box. It's not just for girls either. Boys can also enjoy it with ties, hats, jackets, vests and boots.

- Crayons, pencils and paper should always be available for kids (and it will save your walls and your nerves). They travel well and are inexpensive too. It will do you well to set up a corner somewhere in the house they can access by themselves, and clean up by themselves too.

- If you don't want the mess of paints, try the paint-with-water books. The paint is already on the paper and all you need is a brush and plain water. This is very good for young children.

- Activity books always come in handy. They are cheap, educational and fun. What's not to like? Buy one that is age appropriate.

- Music soothes the savage beast. One of the best purchases I made was buying a cheap (less than $15) plastic tape recorder and player. Kids can learn to appreciate all types of music if they are exposed to a variety early in life. Go to the library and explore different types of music for free. Take advantage of tapes that are accompanied by books to read along with. It's a fun way to introduce young children to the world of reading.

- Use blank tapes for kids to record their own voice. They love playing and listening to themselves singing, reciting or just acting silly.

- Old socks can be turned into hand puppets in a snap. Use a magic marker to make eyes and mouths. If you're more ambitious, sew on button eyes or glue odds and ends for decoration. Or, the kids can make their own using non-toxic marker and glue.

- Kids can paint or color large sheets of cheap newsprint paper. Keep them for wrapping paper. The comics from the newspaper also make good wrapping paper.

- Age appropriate board or card games with the family are good ways to spend time together and encourage interaction with your kids. You may even learn something new about them, and the kids get to see you at play.

- Eight year olds and up may enjoy starting a journal. Self-expression is healthy at any age. All they need is a notebook and privacy (promise them you won't snoop). It could help a teen to explore their emotions and gain personal insight.

- Remember the things you used to like as a kid. Times may have changed, but people haven't. You may be surprised that kids still like puzzles, model kits, jacks, sidewalk chalk, marbles, kites and jump ropes. The important thing is to introduce kids to a variety of activities at a young age. Instill in them the confidence to participate in numerous circumstances when they are willing to follow your lead. They will grow into teens that know they have other options besides hanging on the corner. They may stray for a while, but this foundation will stick with them.

- Sports equipment is expensive. Consignment shops are a great source to tap for them. You know how fickle kids can be about starting and stopping new hobbies. This is the graveyard of forgotten sports items, and at least 50% off retail. Because kids grow so quickly, many of these items are in very good condition. Don't deny your child the opportunity to participate in sports because the equipment is too expensive.

Another option is to ask other parents from the older teams if they are willing to part with some old, unused sports gear.

- Baby items are also a great find at the consignment shops. It's the same theory, the baby grows so quickly, and those items hardly get a change to get used. From bassinets to snow suits, these stores are usually chock full of baby things.

- Buy your kids the same colored gloves. If one gets lost, you'll have another to match. The same goes for socks. Plain white and solid colored socks with no identifying stripes or patterns will keep you from hunting for matches all the time.

- Have an indoor picnic. It's a fun family activity in the winter or when the weather's not cooperating. Spread a blanket or tablecloth on the floor, bring over the radio and have lemonade and sandwiches. If you're ambitious, fry chicken or make barbecue in the oven. Easiest way, order a pizza or bucket of chicken and chow down!

- Start your kids early in life drinking water, especially in hot weather. From infancy on up, water is essential for good health, and our kids don't drink enough of it. We get hit with a double whammy of the expense of juices and sugary drinks and improper hydration of the body. Don't make the mistake of getting your kids hooked on syrupy drinks with no nutritional value. Even too much juice can cause problems, from upset stomachs to allergic reactions. A recent study in *Pediatrics* journal revealed that 12 to 30 ounces a day of juice is considered too much. That is as little as 2 cups. They claim it may cause malnutrition, because it curbs the appetite and displaces calories from other foods. Don't get me wrong; I'm not saying you shouldn't enjoy an occasional fruit juice or soda, but using water as your staple beverage is better for your body and your budget. Start the water habit in your family right now. From constipation to acne, water can do wonders for your health. Yes, and the same thing go for us adults! Next time you eat out, look at how much you spent on beverages compared to your meal.

- I've switched from the more expensive juice boxes and bought reusable plastic drink containers. In the summer, I fill the containers and freeze (only fill ¾ full). When they bring their lunch to camp or school, the frozen juice keeps their food cool. By the time they eat their lunch, it's thawed enough for drinking.

- Flavored seltzer is a hit with my kids and me. It does have flavor, but no calories or sugar. It's fizzy, and a slice of lemon or a cherry makes it even more fun. It's also much cheaper than soda.

- Make the foods you want your kids to eat attractive. Children can be very suspicious about new foods. My kids won't grab a carrot from the fridge when they want to snack, but I can entice them to eat healthier. I make a platter of celery and carrot sticks, sliced fresh fruit (do use lemon juice to keep them from going brown) and maybe some cheese and crackers. Sometimes I add peanut butter or fat-free ranch dressing for dipping. Watch it disappear!

- Begin early and continue to be a part of your children's education all the way to the end. School is a partnership between student, their family and the teacher. Most parents start off excited as the little one goes off to Kindergarten looking so cute in their new outfits. Back to school nights for them through to second and third grade are pretty robust. As the kids get in higher grades, parents slowly drop out of sight. I imagine this happens because we can get comfortable, feel we know how the system works and think our kids can handle school on their own. In reality, the opposite is actually true. As your kids mature and enter middle and high school, potential life-changing decisions are being made and attitudes are being shaped. Hopefully these issues will be guided and discussed with the family.

However, you have to be a player on the team to participate in the game. Do your kids think you are on their team?

- Make use of your local library. It's a safe, fun place to be. Libraries are not only a storehouse of information, but they provide lots of free perks. In addition to the usual book borrowing, videos and audio tapes are also available. Most libraries have computers for members to use. They host special events like story readings by authors, movie showings, educational offerings and computer activities. Stop by and pick up flyers and brochures on what your library has to offer. It's never too late, but if you start when the kids are young, it will become a lifetime habit.

- It amazes me that parents don't realize their son or daughter is not going to graduate a week before the event. Usually, it's these parents that are ready to run up the school, cuss out the teacher (whom they are seeing for the first time), and blame everyone but themselves for their child's failure. Parents are just as much responsible for a student's success in school as the teacher. Early and consistent parental participation produces successful students. It's as simple as that. If the system is faulty, join in and do something to make it better. If you're not part of the solution, you're part of the problem. Join in with other interested parents and gain strength in your numbers. We can make a difference in our kids' lives, but we have to do it with action, not lip service. I know we are all busy trying to make a living, but if you don't pay your dues now, you'll pay them later. And it won't be pleasant. You may not be able to attend every PTA meeting and school event, but I found that if you show interest, most teachers are very willing to make special arrangements for parents and guardians. Bottom line, when you show that education is important to you, it will be important to your child.

- I have found it easier all the way around to require a set amount of time each weekday for study and homework. This eliminates rushing through their assignments or coming home announcing they don't have any homework. If they know study time is mandatory regardless, there will be less reason to shirk their responsibilities. Keep activity books handy for younger kids, novels or interesting magazines and books for older kids. When they really don't have any homework, they can always read. You can be creative of how you want to fill that time. Perhaps instrument practice, story writing or a hobby.

- Win the clothes war. Don't fall into the advertiser's ploys that pressure parents to buy children expensive, name-brand clothes. Help your kids to understand that clothes don't change who they are nor do they define them. Arm your family with information about market strategies and who really wins this war. Discuss costs, style options and why they think they've just gotta have it (whatever "it" may be). It's too bad that parents are often the culprits that plant these thought seeds. They have already bought into the idea owning certain products make you a hipper, better person or will hook you up with someone that's cooler, better looking or richer. The parents themselves set the stage for their kids to buy into that crap. How many tots do you see that are barely walking sporting a pair of Nike's and designer jeans. Don't they look cute? Soon that cute kid is 6 foot tall, wearing size 15 sneakers that cost $200 a pair. How cute is that now? Too many of us choose clothes over computers or college.

- Back to school shopping can be a drain on your emotions and wallet. Before hitting the malls, join forces with your kids and investigate their existing clothes. Have a home fashion show and make decisions on what goes, is in, out or indifferent. Make a comprehensive list of what can be bought to stretch and update clothes they still intend to wear. Even though styles change from year to year (why do you think that is?), your kids shouldn't need a complete new wardrobe, unless they've worked and saved money on their own. Peer pressure doesn't have to drive your blood pressure sky high trying to pay for clothes you can't afford.

- Make household finance a family affair. Every resident over the age of five can be a contributor to the home, whether it is helping with chores, service or financial. Family meetings can be the forum for discussing the family finances, goals and personal wishes. Perhaps the family wants to go to Disney for a vacation. Each family member can do something to help this family wish come true. Your son may be able to earn some extra money cutting lawns. Your daughter may be able to make some baby-sitting money. Perhaps, they will forfeit a birthday gift or money in lieu of taking the vacation. The important thing is to include them and ask their opinion. This practice is a constant reality check for you and the kids. It helps them to understand why they sometimes can't get what they want.

- This can also teach kids how to save for the big-ticket items they desire. They'll take better care of it when they get it, and be happier with less. The burden should never be totally on the parents shoulders, whether they can afford it or not. This is a source of knowledge and money management skills for your children that they will never lose. You may be quite surprised how cooperative kids can be when they are included in the decision-making. You don't need to overwhelm your kids with every minor money situation that arises and detail. The simple act of viewing them as team members with valid ideas and thoughts means they are valued in the home. Self-esteem gets built and they have the confidence to achieve. The family bonds become stronger because trust is being built.

- Evaluate what values you are passing along to your kids. Are you obsessed with material things? Do you spend your precious time with them? As parents, it's very important to make our kids aware of the value of nonperishable goods. No, I'm not talking food-stuff—I'm talking about the stuff we are made of. Valuables that can never be taken away from them. A good self-image, strong body, smart mind and empowered spirit. These are priceless gifts that don't cost money. You will pay with sweat and tears, though, and it won't happen overnight. It's daily reaffirming that gets the job done. Over and over we must show them how important they are to us, to their people, to the world and to God. We are commanded by God to provide our kids with constant love, praise, reassurance, guidance and discipline.

- Bartering is an African tradition that is still invaluable today. Simply it is folks exchanging services rather than paying for them. Sharing tasks helps all involved to juggle their busy schedules. For instance, don't pay for a baby-sitter; find other parents who are interested in swapping dates. Of course, know the people you are dealing with. Start with friends and family and get a wider circle to draw from through word of mouth and referrals. Perhaps you know an elderly person who is a great seamstress, but can't get out to the market or doctor when she needs to. You could take her where she needs to go, and she could return the favor with a sewing project like drapes or slipcovers. Some examples of services that are easily bartered are cooking, cleaning, carpooling, sewing, baby-sitting, general errand or grocery shopping or household repair. Start a trend in your community. Start talking to neighbors, family members, coworkers and other parents for suggestions on how to best utilize this tool. You'll gain an extra benefit by getting to know those who live around you. Communities that share and care for one another become prosperous and powerful.

- Worried about the state of your neighborhood? Community-minded parents can get together and form "safe houses". Create a schedule and list of home where it's safe for your kids to drop by if necessary. Just think, you may get enough people involved to take back control of your streets.

- Support and patronize your neighborhood endeavors. Businesses owned by folks that live in your community are more likely to hire local people and keep up with any special needs in the area. If I hear, "Oh, his/her (meaning Black businesses) stuff ain't as good as so and so" (meaning some other race) one more time, I'll scream!! The truth be told, most people haven't even given the brother or sister a chance. Many don't even bother to go into the store to see what is being offered. The gossip and envy circulates and spreads like wildfire. The same folks will be upset and ready to riot when another ethnic group comes into the community and sets up shop, though. It's absolutely ludicrous. Tony Brown reports that African-Americans only pass on a pitiful 3% of their spending with other Black businesses. When we don't support our community, we're not supporting ourselves. Let's get past the jealousy and realize that we're all in this together.

- **Invest in Higher Education.** Start saving for your child's higher education as early in their life as possible. It will cost you less if you begin when your child is young, because the invested money will have more time to earn the most interest. There are many different avenues to affording a college education. Grants and scholarships, sometimes known as "gift aid," are forms of financial aid without repayment requirements. They are available from a variety of sources, including federal and state governments. They are also available from private sources, such as employers, professional associations, and educational institutions. Some grants and scholarships are based on financial need, others are awarded based on achievement, religious affiliation, ethnicity, memberships, hobbies, or special interests. The key to finding scholarships is to start early and search diligently. It's equally important to be on the lookout for scholarship scams.

A part of your savings plan may include US EE Savings Bonds. No state or local tax is due on the interest these bonds earn. In addition, some investors will not have to pay federal tax on the interest earned if the bonds are purchased in the parents' names and the bonds are used to pay college tuition. The bonds must be redeemed (cashed in) in the year the tuition is paid, and you must meet the income requirements. The income limits are periodically adjusted. See your tax advisor or local bank to find out if you qualify.

Go on-line for lots of information on scholarships. There is a ton of money available, especially for minorities. If you don't have your own computer or access to one, visit your local library. They have computers with internet access available for use by anyone with a library card. Check out www.Scholarships.com, or *www.finaid.org* for a free college scholarship search and financial aid resource. Money should be the last reason your son or daughter doesn't attend a higher learning institution. Enter the keyword "scholarship' or 'financial aid' into your browsers search engine and you will see the thousands of sites that are looking for scholarship recipients. Take your time, print out the information that interests you, fill out the forms and I guarantee success. Make sure your son or daughter is involved and an active participant in this quest. You are going to need their help and the bottom line is if they are truly interested in attending a secondary school, they have to be willing to do whatever is necessary to get there.

Chapter 6: On the J.O.B.

I find it so ironic that getting a job immediately means you'll have to spend some money. Sure, you're happy because now you'll be earning some steady money. But now that you're working, you have additional expenses. For starters, you need professional clothing, transportation and lunch money. I've put in over 30 years in the work force, working in various states and job positions. During those years, I've discovered lots of ways to stretch my paycheck to the limit.

The Brown Bag Factor

Taking your lunch to work doesn't always mean brown bagging it. Yes, you will save some money, but sandwiches can get boring in a hurry. Eating out on a regular basis can cost you a fortune, and it's not just lunch. Think about how much money you spend only on coffee or soda each day. Machines sodas cost from 75 cents to 1.50, compared with 35 to 50 cents from the supermarket. A twelve ounce jar of brand name instant coffee will cost your around 6 dollars (at Walmart) and makes about 180 six ounce cups of coffee. Buy that many cups of coffee at $1 a cup, and you've spent $180.00. Just by toting in your instant coffee has saved you $174! Imagine that.

Microwave technology makes it a whole lot easier to bring leftovers to work than it ever was before. Microwaves weren't even invented yet when I started working, but I still found a way to get over. Back then, hot pots were popular in college dorms and offices. They were used to heat water for instant coffee or tea, or make soup or warm up last night's dinner. Hot pots are still available today and costs under $20. They plug into a standard outlet and look like a miniature coffee pot. If you happen to work at a facility that doesn't provide an eating facility or service, you might want to give the hot pot a try. Make sure you read all the documentation that comes with the hot pot to insure you use the product safely.

The following items travel well, stay fresh and are easy to prepare. Keep non-perishables in your desk, cabinet or carry a lunch box. Reusable ice packs are still available for insulated lunch bags to keep your food cold if need be. If you happen to work at a site with refrigerators, microwaves or a full service cafeteria, you can be even more creative. Watch the money you save grow fast. Remember, just by bringing coffee, you're saving about 35 dollars per month right off the bat! There's no doubt you're going to start saving fast, just make sure you have a plan for those savings, so you get the most satisfaction possible. Start seeing yourself there to keep motivation high. Stock your desk or carry in and reap the rewards.

Below is a list of items you can pick and choose from. They are tried and tested.

* can opener

* fork, spoon, knife

* Reusable, microwave-able dishes or plastic ware (cup, bowl and/or small plate)

* Canned tuna, salmon, soup, beans

* Ramen noodles

* Instant coffee, tea bags, hot chocolate packets

* Fresh fruit

* Powder drink mixes (like sweetened kool-aid, crystal light or ice tea)

* Crackers, cookies

* Baked goods like bread, rolls, Danish or donuts

* Individual condiment packets (saved from take-out orders): mus-tard, mayo, relish, soy sauce, salsa, barbecue sauce or ketchup

* small container of liquid soap (or use liquid soap from the bath-room)

You may feel like you're turning your desk into a pantry, and you're right, it's very similar. Of course, I don't expect you to bring in all the items on the list. Please, don't bust into work tomorrow and start cram-ming your drawers with food or set up a kitchen display on your desk. You are still at work, and bringing any food from home should be done with discretion and professionalism.

Take into consideration where you work, the location of your desk, your job title and office rules and regulations. Do you work in an area that is exposed to customers, your boss or other coworkers who could right-fully complain? Thrifty Sister doesn't want you to lose your job trying to save some bucks, okay? That's called going nowhere fast. However, it is the law that you are entitled to take lunch during an eight-hour workday. You can bring your fixings into the designated area and have your lunch there.

I seem to recall that at some jobs I held, there were always a few folks snickering behind my back when I'd pull out my can of soup. However, they were taking the bus to work and I was saving for a car. They'd all be eyeing me as they sucked down burgers and fries while I patiently warmed up my leftovers. They almost choked, though, when I pulled up in my new car. Had the nerve to ask me for a ride, too! I don't know about you, but I felt like eating in-house was a small price to pay, and it wasn't a drastic sacrifice. It wasn't like I didn't eat at all to save for the car. I saved from $5 to $10 dollars per day. Multiply that times 20 days in an average month, and what do you get? That comes to 100 to 200 dollars per month. Can you think of a few good uses for that kind of money?

I'll bet your didn't know you were spending that much…and just on lunch and coffee!

Movin' On Up

I know too many brothers and sisters who are working more than one job. Honestly, I admire their dedication and desire to succeed. It also saddens me to see how hard they're working just to make ends meet. The two or more job syndrome may get the bills paid, but it can also work against you. First, it takes precious time away from the important people in our lives, especially our kids. Secondly, it wears you down physically, stresses you out and drains your mental faculties.

Really think about it, is that second job worth the sacrifices it forces you to make? Neglecting your own health and the people who love and need you can cost you big in the long run. A better scenario would be to earn as much money at one job as you make with both combined, right? If you could focus on the first job and get as much mileage as possible from it, you may be able to do without a second one. It is possible if you know how to work the system.

Right off the bat, I admit that we Blacks get hired for less money and work harder, yet get fewer promotions and raises. Some years ago, I taught 30 women word processing and typesetting through a city-funded job-training program in Texas. The women were screened through Social Services and promised jobs at the end of their six-month training session. Their ages ranged from 21 to 65, mostly Black and Hispanic, and one or two Whites. It was a real eye-opener to me to see with very interesting and diverse group in action. I saw first hand how small traits we ourselves consider insignificant are quite pronounced to others. It was easy to see why this group was having such a hard time getting and keeping jobs. Skill level was the least of their problems.

First of all, some sisters have an attitude problem. A hostile attitude that burns from within and scorches anyone in its path. This attitude is a front, a means to convey they don't take nobody's stuff. That may work 'round the way, but we've got to learn to keep that attitude in check. When that attitude gets carried into an interview, the only stuff they won't be taking is that job, because they won't get hired! About half of my class had this problem.

Then there were a few students, from the very first day, acted like they were doing me a favor by showing up to class. Others would come dressed like they were going out clubbing, while others came looking as poor and as downtrodden as they felt. I could tell by the end of the first week who was destined for failure if they didn't make some changes. How we carry ourselves, what we say and how we say it has tremendous impact on how successful we'll be in the workplace. Yes, clothes do play a part in your game plan, but in most cases it won't be the main reason you get a job or promotion. Don't rely too heavily on appearance and place more emphasis on performance.

The next personality type were those with the workhorse syndrome. So eager to please they became doormats. In their quest for recognition they took on more than their fair share of work. Instead of being recognized, they only became weary and resentful. Their peers would state, "Oh, she likes all that work!" Rarely does this type person get promotions of any real substance. Because they are overloaded with assignments, there is no time to schmooze with management. Physically they always seemed disheveled and tired. Someone else (with more time and savvy) usually takes some, if not all the credit for his or her work.

Women's Weekly did a study recently and reported that employees who avoid thoughts that reflect negative emotion get promoted more frequently. Positive thinking and self-talk can change the way your feel about yourself. The better you feel about yourself, the more confidence you will have. The more confidence, the more risks you'll be willing to take and more job opportunities will come your way.

Take the steps to increase your salary where you are now or through new employment. The obvious benefit is you'll have more time. Visualize yourself five or ten years down the road. Ask yourself these questions.

How long do you intend to work two jobs? What goals do you plan to achieve through working two jobs? (In other words, why do you need to work two jobs in the first place?) How long will you physically be able to continue on this level? How much of an impact are the long hours having on your personal and/or family life? If you don't care much for the answers that loom before you, take a look at three ideas that may work for you.

1. Seek Out Education: Getting a degree can increase your salary big time. Going back to school doesn't have to mean long hours at an expensive university or taking on big loans. Your company may provide tuition refund or some sort of incentive for broadening your knowledge base. Let management know you are interested in gaining new skills. Visit your Human Resources department or call Personnel and find out all the details about your education benefits or career development.

Simply taking advantage of seminars, workshops and individual courses without the intention of earning a degree is another way to show you are on the lookout for job growth. All you have to do is share your intention with another coworker and ask them to keep it quiet. The news will get around fast. Showing initiative and interest in new projects displays your potential to your superiors and gets you noticed. Once you see opportunities that interest you, schedule an appointment with your boss and talk candidly about your goals within the company. Make sure you've done your homework and get all the details about any new activity in the office. It never hurts to go directly to the one who holds the purse strings. Next time an opening comes available, your name may be in the forefront of management's mind.

Another education vehicle is distance learning. On-line classes through the Internet are fast becoming a booming business. Companies are joining forces to provide education to their employees at a fraction of the cost of brining in traditional classroom instruction. There are credited and non-credited courses available through the Internet that can earn you a degree or certification. Ziff-Davis University is one of the leaders in "e-learning". If you have access to the Internet, get on your browser and search it out.

2. Turn Your Talents Into a Side Business: Another income booster is to extend your skills to a home business. If you are handy, perhaps you can take on a neighbor's home improvement project such as wallpapering or stenciling. If you're an accountant, work in billing, or are just good with numbers, you could do taxes or bookkeeping for a store in your neighborhood. Crafts, gift baskets or sewing projects can bring in additional money. If you're a great cook, there are opportunities in catering or cake baking. Love plants? Try your hand at floral arrangements or propagating houseplants. Write out what you would like to do and put together a plan. Test out the waters. Start with a friend or relative and see what it takes to complete an assignment. Get one client or sale and see how it goes. Tell everyone you know about your venture when you're sure. Make up business cards and flyers and give them out. There are no limits, except the ones you put on yourself.

3. Make a career change. Check out Employment/Temporary Agencies: Now called "outsourcing", this fast-growing business practice has become a mainstay of many corporations. Because I've lived in many states, I've used this vehicle for quick employment wherever I go. I feel the pro's definitely outweigh the cons with agencies. If you shop around, I'm sure you can find one that will fit your needs. Some agencies provide medical and retirement benefits, some are temporary-to-permanent positions, some offer long-term assignments, and some simply pay a good hourly wage with no benefits whatsoever. The positives you can get from agency work are numerous enough to list:

- Free computer training on various office software.

- A chance to try out different positions to see what suits you.

- Get your foot in the door of more companies (Fortune 500 types) that you otherwise would have no access to.

- Test out a job before you commit to it permanently, should the opportunity arise. Both sides get to take a look at each other before the deal is made, increasing the probability that this job offers growth potential.

- Gain new skills

- Meet new professional people to network with

- More freedom to choose days or hours that works for you

- Flexibility to pick and choose assignments that appeal to you

- Competitive salary

- Long and short-term opportunities

The main downside of working through agencies is the medical and/or retirement benefits can be lacking or nonexistent. You may not get sick or vacation time. More agencies are providing a comprehensive benefits package because the demand for contract personnel is growing. If benefits are the main ingredient in your employment formula, don't write off agencies yet. You may want to consider taking a short assignment, just to gain the skills you need to compete in the job market. Call around and ask in a pleasant, professional manner to be mailed an information packet or schedule an appointment.

Chapter 7: Crib Notes

When you step through your front door, your home should be a haven from the wacky world outside. Making your house a home doesn't have to cost a fortune. Since housing expenses take up the largest chunk of our budget, why not make the most of it? These money and space-saving ideas can transform even the smallest apartment into a home you can be proud of, and enjoy living in!

- If your place is itching for a makeover, get new ideas by looking through decorating magazines. Those magazines can be expensive so don't forget about your local library. Visit furniture stores to see room arrangements, color schemes and accessory choices. Always keep in mind your family's living style. You may think white couches may look lovely in the showroom, but what will they look like after a year in your home?

- Paint the room. Nothing changes a room more dramatically for the least money than paint. Do it yourself and save big on labor costs. Always use high-quality paint. It's well worth paying a bit more because you'll get better results in less time and the finish will be longer lasting. You don't want to have to paint again in a year or two...where's the savings in that? There are all kinds of painting techniques, depending on how much time you are willing to spend. Go to your local hardware or paint store and pick up some free manufacturer's pamphlets. Don't be afraid to try something new. You can always paint over it if you don't like it. If you're feeling timid, experiment on one wall as an accent.

- Paint stores often have discounted leftover custom-colored paint. Ask the sales person, they may not be out in plain sight. If you like the colors, you've got yourself quality paint at 30 to 70% off retail! Always have your room dimensions written down, and buy enough to allow for a little leftover for touchups.

- Paint a level line on the outside of the paint can. You'll know at a glance how much paint is in it and the color.

- Instead of tape, wrap aluminum foil around doorknobs and other odd shapes before painting around them. You won't have to worry about excess paint on the tape that makes it difficult to remove. Also, aluminum foil is reusable!

- Use strips of wet newspaper instead of tape when painting window trim. It comes off quickly and easily. No glue residue!

- Add a border after painting and you've got a custom look without a lot of wallpapering and work. Lengthen a wall by adding the border to the top of the wall butt to the ceiling. Break up a long wall by applying the border across the middle of the wall. Make a short wall look taller by adding the border ¾ way up the wall.

- Spruce up an old, but still sturdy couch, love seat or chair. The new furniture covers are a far cry from the old "furniture throws". The new covers are shaped and tuck-able and come in a variety of colors and prints.

- Make quick slipcovers by covering a dark, heavy chair or sofa with a colorful quilt or African mud cloth. No sewing necessary, just toss it over and tuck in the edges. You want to make sure you use fabric that is heavy enough to stay put. Something like a sheet or table-cloth would be too thin and slippery.

- Mix a few good furniture pieces with accessories from flea markets or tag sales. These are great places to shop for unusual, cheap accessories and knick-knacks that reflect who you are. They add charm and personalize your home. The quality pieces last a long time and add classic character to any room.

- Be ready to save. Keep index cards with measurements of windows, walls and rooms. Ever see a great find, but are scared to purchase cause your not sure it will fit? For windows you need to measure the width and height of the window itself. Then a measurement from the top of the window to the floor. For blinds or shades you'll need an inside window measurement.

- Inexpensive blinds and toppers are $5 each and easy to install. There are light filtering and room darkening features and come in a variety of color.

- Lamps can be recycled. Simply changing the lampshade gives an old lamp new life. Go one step further by covering the base with material. Add a cultural flair by using African mud cloth. Tie up the top with cord or a jute rope. This no-sew idea is easy and drastically changes the look of the lamp.

- Pillows add flair and interest to any room. You can make quick ones from odd or old pillowcases that no longer have matching sheets. Simply add stuffing (use cut up old clothes, old stockings, pieces of foam or fill from old pillows), cut, tuck the top and top stitch the end. Add pillows to beds, couches, chairs, or even stack on the floor. This is a great project for the whole family. See who can come up with the most creative pillow.

- Buy an extra pair of sheets to make matching curtains for a bedroom. They're a lot less expensive than ready-made coordinates. If you can sew a straight line, you can make curtains.

- Keep your linens organized by storing the sheet sets inside the coordinating pillowcase.

- Baskets make great organizers. They come in all shapes, sizes and colors and look great anywhere. Visit craft stores for the best prices.

- Buy bad art for the frame. I've gotten nice frames from discount stores with bad art. Framed cartoon characters and ugly prints are usually marked down. Make sure the frame is one you can take apart without destroying it. If it's a really cheap frame, it may be all one piece. In that case, don't bother buying it. Great frames can be found at garage sales. Seems every family had someone who tried their hand at painting, so of course they have to frame those masterpieces nicely!

- Frame pretty pictures from photography magazines or National Geographic. Dried or pressed leaves or flowers arranged on pretty wrapping paper make a nice display. What about the doodling of your artistic son or daughter.

- Set aside an afternoon and paint your own masterpiece. You don't have to be an artist to do it. Simply buy a stretched canvas or canvas board. Buy acrylic paints in the color scheme of your room and a few cheap brushes. Put on some mood music and create your own abstract design. Splatter, streak, spray and stroke till your heart's content until you're satisfied with the results.

- Stretch an ethnic print or pretty floral fabric over a canvas stretcher and hang. Instant art!

Most apartment dwellers need more space than what they have. These space saving ideas are inexpensive and innovative.

- Use a trunk or chest for a coffee table and store goods inside.

- Make this end table. Top an old plastic garbage can with a plywood or chipboard round and top with fabric. Storage space inside the garbage can.

- Make or buy a bench with storage space under the seat. Use these instead of regular chairs at your eating table.

- Tower bookshelves. Thin enough to fit in the narrowest space, but tall enough to hold quantity.

- Over the commode shelf. This is great, especially if you don't have a linen closet or a medicine cabinet.

- If your bathroom sink is minus a vanity and has ugly piping exposed, take an old sheet or shower curtain and make a skirt. This can be done easily with Velcro strips glued to the outer edge of the sink sides. Or sew elastic onto the fabric edge and slip it around the sink base. Not only are you covering an eyesore, you can now store extra items under the sink skirt.

- Cabinets that go all the way up to the ceiling eliminate wasted wall space in a small kitchen. If your cabinets don't reach the top, how about using that space to display collectibles or for storage. Baskets can hold your stuff and look nice too.

Put the "You" Back in Utility

We trust that our lights will come on with a flick of the switch, and water will come out when we turn on the faucet. Because we've become so comfortable with these commodities, we forget how much we're paying for those conveniences. We get careless with their usage. Conserving energy will reduce our utility bills and helps our environment. The trick to reducing energy use in your home is to make small

changes that save big. This way, everybody wins. If we all make a conscious effort to conserve, there may be some natural resources left for
our grandkids to enjoy.

- Check windows and doors for heat loss. Inspect walls, floors and
  ceilings for gaps, then weather-strip or caulk.

- Turn down your thermostat in the winter. Any temperature higher
  than 68 degrees increases your heating expenses 3% per degree.

- Turn up your thermostat a few degrees in the summer. This slight
  adjustment won't raise your blood pressure, but it will reduce your
  overall energy bill.

- In summer, vacuum the air conditioner filters once a month to get
  maximum air flow and reduce pollutants and dust.

- Install a programmable thermostat. They don't cost a whole lot
  (starting at $25), and considering the amount you'll save, consider
  them downright cheap. My family experienced a 25% reduction in
  our energy bill immediately. No one has to remember to turn down
  the heat at night or before leaving the house. It's easy to set auto-
  matically, with an override for off-schedule days.

- Lower the wattage of light bulbs where you don't need that much
  light like closets and hallways.

- Turn off your dishwasher's drying cycle. This cycle is almost as long
  as the wash and uses extra power to heat the air. All you have to do
  is open it up to dry (which I love to do in the winter cause all the
  steam that billows out adds some humidity to the air).

- Get the most heat out of your furnace and keep it running at peak
  efficiency by changing the filter once a month. It's easy to do; most
  simply slide in and out, but please read the directions anyway! Keep

an old one around to take to the store with you to ensure you buy the right replacement.

Keep Good Records

If you don't have proof, you can't win a case. Whether it's an accident in your home and the need to file a claim or cover damage or loss, you'll need supporting evidence and records. Keep these important papers in a fire-proof strongbox:

- Insurance policies

- Mortgage deeds and property records

- Stocks, bonds

- Birth certificates

- Marriage license

- Passports

- Tax returns (keep for 7 years)

- Auto titles

- Warranties and receipts on major appliances

You're Buggin'

We hate the pesky bugs, but who wants to inhale toxic sprays and powders? If you have kids or pets, you just can't risk using hazardous products in your home. Try these environmentally safe home remedies to shoo them away.

- Repel ants by sprinkling cinnamon under cabinets, around windowsills and across door thresholds. Place cinnamon sticks wherever ants hang out. You may have to repeat this a few times at first, but when they are gone, they're gone for good!

- An alternate method to ant reduction is to use a mixture of water and lemon juice on the doorways and windowsills, or use in conjunction with the cinnamon sticks.

- Roaches have been around since the beginning of time and are even expected to survive a nuclear holocaust. Here are a few tips for keeping roaches on the run. Clean out all your cabinets and throw out any food that shows signs of infestation. Wash down the inside of cabinets and doors with a nontoxic garden insecticide. Transfer all boxed foods to seal able, plastic containers, storage bags or glass jars. Apply a fine layer of boric acid under sinks and baseboards. Place bottle caps filled with boric acid in corners of cabinets.

- Repel wasps and bees by placing inexpensive toilet bowl deodorizers wherever they gather. Hang one on your outdoor garbage cans. Take off the wire and place in pretty baskets. Place anywhere you don't want bees around, like your picnic table, porch or patio.

- Keep a spray bottle with water close by in the house and yard. Spray bees and flies with water. This wets down their wings, making them slower and easier to swat and kill.

- Gnats won't swarm you if you rub vanilla extract on your skin.

- Wear a bandanna if you're working in the yard. Gnats seem to love the scents of the products we apply to our hair. Spray it first with garden insecticide and let dry before tying it on your head.

- Citronella candles and torches repel mosquitoes and gnats. Set them out in close proximity to where the people are.

- Rub white vinegar directly onto the skin to repel bugs and keep them from biting.

- Got bit or stung anyway? Make a paste with meat tenderizer and water to take out the sting. Witch Hazel, ice or ammonia will numb the area and take the sting out.

- Place fresh basil in your bowl of fruit and you won't have to worry about fruit flies.

- A stick of spearmint gum in your flour and sugar canisters will keep mealy bugs away.

Potpourri

Flowers and plants are a great decorating tool, especially when money is tight. They can be a focal point of a room or hide an eyesore. Plants improve the quality of indoor air. If your place lacks natural light, a plant light will do the trick while adding drama to the room. Even a regular light bulb is better than no light and will sustain a low-light loving plant. Silk plants and flowers are practically maintenance free; just dust every now and them. Anyway you decide to display them, you can't go wrong with plants. Here are some tips on keeping them around as long as possible.

- Floral arrangements don't have to be kept in vases. Anything that can hold water can be used. Colorful, but chipped or cracked cups, pitchers and bowls that you can't use but love too much to throw out are perfect receptacles. They make wonderful holders for fresh, dried or silk flower arrangements.

- Old pots and pans work well for outdoor planters. The old fashioned, speckled black turkey roasting pans are nice and big enough to make a spectacular patio planter. It can be kept natural or spruced up with acrylic paint. Add some Styrofoam peanuts in the bottom for drainage (and to keep the weight as light as possible). Add potting soil and plants of your choice.

- When you receive flowers, re-cut flower stems on an angle under running water before transferring them to a vase. The stems suck up a measurable amount of water during this first cut. Shortly afterward, water bubbles form on the stem and reduce water absorption.

- Cut fresh flowers from your garden before or after the heat of the day. Bring a pail of water with you to put them in immediately after cutting to reduce wilting.

- Strip the leaves from stems of flowers that fall beneath the water. This will keep the water fresher longer without leaves decomposing and contaminating the vase water.

- Keep a dried floral arrangement from shedding by spraying with 2 or 3 coats of hair spray.

- General flower food: 2 tablespoons each vinegar and sugar added to 1 quart of water.

- Flowers will stay fresh for weeks if you add a capful of bleach to the vase water.

- Use a half and half mixture of water and lemon-lime soda for longer lasting roses.

- Use a clear, plastic straw to help a bent, leggy stem stay straight in your flower arrangement.

- Houseplants die most frequently from over watering and subsequent root rot. You'll be better off watering less if you're not sure it needs it.

- Occasionally rotate your houseplants ¼ turn clockwise to the light source for even growth.

- Eggshells, once thoroughly dried, make a good fertilizer for plants. Crush the shells into small pieces and add directly to the soil, working ¼ inch deep into the dirt. Another option is to simply add them to your watering can. Allow the water to sit for a day or overnight. Keep in a cool, dark place and replace the shells once a month. Whenever you water, the plants will receive a nutritious drink.

The Clean Up Woman

We love our homes to sparkle, but who wants to do the back breaking work to keep it that way? Adding insult to injury is the fact that all those cleaning products cost a fortune! Here's how you can save the hefty price of cleaning products. I've found a few basics ingredients that have multiple uses. Save plastic spray bottles of the products you have now to house your new and improved mixtures. These basic substances not only cost less, but are environmentally-friendly and can take care of most any cleaning dilemma: Ammonia, Baking Soda, Bleach, Lemon, Rubbing Alcohol, Salt, Vinegar.

NOTE: Never ever mix Ammonia and Bleach; they cause a toxic odor and fumes that is very hazardous to humans and animals.

- Gravity is the basis for the old phrase, "clean from top to bottom". Use this concept all over the house for time-effective cleaning. Always start from the highest areas of any room, working your way down to the floor. You don't want dirt settling on an area you just cleaned. Think about it, if you clean from the bottom up, what will happen? All the dirt you raise will find it's way downward. Stairs too, so that all the dirt falls down to where you have not cleaned yet.

- Toilet Cleaner: Add ¼ cup bleach to the toilet water, scrub with a toilet brush dusted with baking soda.

- All Purpose Cleaner #1: Add ½ cup ammonia, 1/3 cup vinegar, 2 tablespoons baking soda to 1 gallon water.

- All Purpose Cleaner #2: Add ½ cup dishwasher detergent, 1/3 cup bleach to 1 gallon of water.

- Furniture Polish: Mix 1 tablespoon lemon juice (extract) with 1-quart vegetable oil.

- Silver Polish: Soak silver in 1 pint boiling water with 1-tablespoon baking soda and 1 inch strip of aluminum foil.

- Moth Balls: Make sachets (or use your old stockings) using cedar chips, lavender flowers, peppercorns, dried tobacco or equal parts of dried rosemary and mint leaves.

- Don't throw away those perfume samples that come in the magazines. Keep your bathroom smelling fresh by inserting the sampler cards inside a new toilet paper roll. With each use the roll will release a sweet scent.

- Treated Furniture Polish: ¾ cup vinegar, 1 ¼ cup linseed oil, and ¾ cup rubbing alcohol. Keep in a plastic quart container. Shake well before using.

- Carpet Freshener: Sprinkle dry cornstarch or baking soda on carpet. Let sit ½ to one hour. Vacuum up.

- General Disinfectant: Mix ½ cup borax to 1 gallon of water.

- Drain Cleaner: Combine 1 cup boiling water to ¼ cup baking soda with 2 oz. vinegar. Pour down drain. Let sit for 10 minutes, then force down with plunger. Flush with hot water. Repeat monthly to keep drain running freely.

- Window Cleaner: ¼ cup vinegar with 1 quart of water. Add a capful of alcohol. Pour into spray bottle. Bonus, the alcohol will keep bathroom mirrors from fogging up. For added protection, you can wipe the mirror with a cloth dampened with alcohol.

- If your carpet is new, you should avoid shampooing it for as long a possible. Frequent vacuuming is the best way to keep carpets clean and new looking. However, once your carpet has passed it's prime and is screaming for a wash, try the cleaner below.

- Carpet Cleaner: Mix ½ cup powdered detergent with 1 gallon of water. Rinse with vinegar and water, one cup vinegar to 1 gallon of water. For spot cleaning, reduce amounts to 1/8 cup detergent to 1 quart of water for washing and ¼ cup vinegar to 1 quarter of water for rinsing. The secret to keeping the carpet clean is to remove any soapy residue, which actually attracts more dirt to the area you just cleaned. Vinegar and water helps to remove that soapy residue on the carpet.

- Carpet Stain Remover: Good old shaving cream! Foam it on, brush over stain, let dry and vacuum up.

- Remove gum from carpet: Harden the gum with an ice cube, then pick off as much of the gum as possible, using a butter knife. Wipe off any excess with a cloth dampened with lighter fluid.

- Wallpaper Remover: Spray old wallpaper with a mixture of 2/3-cup hot water and 1/3 cup liquid fabric softener. Let sit for 20 to 30 minutes, and then peel off the paper.

- Floor Wax Remover: Mix 1-cup ammonia, ¼ cup baking soda, and ¾ cup vinegar with 1 gallon of water. Rinse with clear water.

- Remove stale odors from plastic containers. Place crumpled newspaper and a tablespoon of baking soda inside. Seal with the top and let set for a couple of days. Remove paper, wash container and rinse thoroughly.

- Cooking odors on your hands can be removed with lemon juice or a rind.

- Garbage Disposal Freshener: Freeze used citrus rinds. Combat odors in the sink by grinding up a rind in the disposal twice a month.

- Cooking Odors: Place old coffee grinds in a saucer on the stove while you cook. The grinds will absorb much of the odor. A bowl of vinegar will also disperse odors.

- Keep jewelry tarnish free. Store jewelry in an airtight plastic bag with a teaspoon of baking soda.

- Add a small piece of charcoal to containers holding silverware. It will prevent rust by absorbing any moisture. If you don't want the charcoal to dirty anything, wrap the charcoal in a swatch of an old stocking.

- A chemical reaction occurs when aluminum foil is placed near silverware and keeps it rust free.

- Clean your sink with table salt before washing vegetables instead of chemicals. It has enough abrasion to cut through hardened foods and salt has a disinfecting quality.

Laundry Daze

At most homes, especially if there are kids, laundry is a never-ending job. The hamper fills up quicker than you can get the clothes clean. Laundry products cost a bundle and get used up fast, so I'm always on the warpath for any shortcut I can get my hands on. Before trying out any solutions on fabrics for the first time, test them out on an inconspicuous place on the garment. Never mix products containing ammonia and bleach. Together they produce toxic fumes and odors that can burn mucus membranes and skin.

- In general, it's better to blot (gently, but firmly dabbing) rather than rub stains.

- Rubbing usually forces the stain deeper into the fabric and spreads it over a wider area.

- Pre-treat a bloodstain by moistening the area with hydrogen peroxide (3%). Launder as usual.

- Got a wine stain on your tablecloth? Drape the tablecloth over the sink with the stain under the faucet. Cover the stain with table salt. Pour boiling water over the stain until is disappears. Launder as usual.

- Wine stains on a garment can be removed with club soda or white vinegar.

- Ink stains on a white shirt will disappear if you spray the area with hair spray, then wipe with liquid dish detergent. Rinse with cold water and launder as usual.

- Oily hair shampoo works as a pre-treat for "ring-around-the-collar".

- Bar laundry soap works better than those expensive stain sticks and sprays and lasts ten times longer. Rub directly on dirty collars, sleeve and stains. If you can't find laundry soap, use a cheap, generic, non-deodorant soap.

- If you notice a stain is still there after washing, re-wash the item before placing the garment in the dryer. Heat tends to set the stain, sometimes permanently.

- Combat perspiration stains. Make a paste of baking soda and water. Press into the stains, and then wash as usual.

- For old perspiration stains on undershirts, soak with white vinegar. For new stains, soak with ammonia. Wash with hot water.

- Energy saver: Do your laundry all at one time, preferably at night or early in the morning. The residual heat in the dryer from the previous load helps dry the next one quicker.

- Instead of washing smelly sneakers and have them tear up in the washer, soak them in 2 parts water to 1 part vinegar for a few hours. Allow to dry in the sun. They'll be clean and odor free!

- Always wash your clothes before packing them away when the seasons change. Oil, stains and body dirt are the food that moths and their young feed upon, resulting in holes in your clothes. Packing up clean clothes greatly reduces the chances that these pests will take up residence there.

- If you use liquid fabric softener and forget to add it to the rinse cycle, try this trick. Add ½ cup liquid fabric softener to a damp washcloth and toss along with the clothes in the dryer. This method can take the place of buying softener sheets and is actually more cost effective.

- Homemade spray starch: Add 1 tablespoon of cornstarch to 3 cups of warm water. Shake well and pour into an old spray bottle. The more cornstarch you add, the stiffer your clothes will be after ironing. After you've found the strength that suits you, write your recipe on the bottle with a permanent marker. Shake well before using.

Afterword

Thrifty Sister wants you to gain control of your finances without sacrificing other important areas of your life. Money will not solve all of life's problems. Allow me to share with you how money fails us when we don't have a proper perspective on life.

Money can buy…
A bed, but not sleep
Books, but not brains
Food, but not appetite
Luxuries, but not culture
A house, but not a home
Medicine, but not health
Amusement, but not happiness
A church, but not heaven
A wedding band, but not a marriage
A crucifix, but not a Savior
And of course, money can't buy you love.

Well, my friends, I hope you are getting the big picture about the art of thrift. It's something we all can do right now, tonight. Take a look around you and do something nice for yourself, or someone else you love. As I make my way through this life I've been blessed with, I am already excited about the next time we may meet. I find that each day is a new opportunity to meet the same old problems in a new way. I really do use thrift in my everyday life, and some ideas not disclosed in this book are so thrifty, even I would classify them as cheap! But that's my prerogative, isn't it? And who knows, one of these days I may be bold enough to share them. In the meantime, take the time to hug someone and spread love to one another. It is God's greatest commandment, and one we can't live without. From me to you, LOVE is the one thing we should never be thrifty about. Share it, spread it around liberally.

Peace to you all,

Thrifty Sister

THE END

Index

G

H

Home
cleaning, 87, 109, 111
decorating, 98, 107
purchasing, 20, 30, 35

I

Interest rates, 22-23
Investment purchases, 6, 9, 43, 60, 62, 88

J

Jell-O, 37, 40, 53, 79
Jewelry cleaner, 109, 111
Juice,
healthy amounts, 82
enhancements, 40, 41, 83
light varieties, 51
Laundry
stain busters, 122, 123
dryer sheets, 113

Leftovers
concepts, 11
containers, 60, 80, 83, 105, 111-112
freezing, 30, 35, 45-49, 59
menu management, 45, 50

M

Magazines, 98
Makeup, 61-62
Meals
exchanging, 87

0-595-20325-6